Practicing Right Relationship

Practicing Right Relationship

Skills for Deepening Purpose, Finding Fulfillment, and Increasing Effectiveness in Your Congregation

Mary K. Sellon
Daniel P. Smith

Herndon, Virginia
www.alban.org

The Alban Institute
2121 Cooperative Way, Suite 100
Herndon, VA 20171-5370

Cover design: Adele Robey, Phoenix Graphics

LIBRARY OF CONGRESS CATALOGING IN PUBLICATION DATA

Sellon, Mary K.
    Practicing right relationship : skills for deepening purpose, finding fulfillment, and increasing effectiveness in your congregation / Mary K. Sellon, Daniel P. Smith.
        p. cm.
    Includes bibliographical references.
    ISBN 1-56699-314-8
    1. Interpersonal relations—Religious aspects—Christianity. I. Smith, Daniel P., 1938- II. Title.

    BV4597.52S45 2004
    253'.2—dc22
                            2004022736

08   07   06   05   VG   2   3   4   5   6   7   8   9   10

Contents

Foreword

One of the painful parts of being a consultant working with congregations is watching "crash-and-burn" pastorates. Sitting with the governing board of a congregation one evening, I watched the pastor stand at the moment the clock struck 9:00 and announce that he didn't know what others would do but he had a family at home and chose not to be absent from them any longer that day. He promptly left. This pastor had attended seminars about self-care and professional boundaries and believed he was setting a healthy example as spiritual leader of this congregation. Somehow he missed the fact that many of the people sitting around the table, me included, also had families at home and yet were attending this evening meeting that he had called. The reason I was asked to work with this congregation was to address the difficulty people had with their pastor, whom they felt did not understand or care for them.

In another situation, I watched as a pastor increasingly lost the support, respect, and finally the participation of a large portion of the congregation's leaders. With a deeply based commitment to social justice, she had received multiple awards and recognitions in seminary for her preaching and passionate leadership. Arriving from seminary at her appointed congregation, she led people into crusades for justice that were important to her but not to the members and that did not match this congregation's gifts, passions, and needs for ministry. True to her crusading nature, she identified all who did not agree with her as resisters and methodically declined to include them in conversations and decision making. Her leadership with that congregation was truly a crash-and-burn experience for her but was even more devastating to the congregation, which is not likely to survive the loss of members that her leadership prompted.

Clearly both of these clergy had leadership skills, personal passions, and deep faith commitments. But both also stand as strong testament to the truth to which Dan Smith and Mary Sellon point: Leadership is not a matter of using certain skills and implementing particular practices, nor is it about being right. Leadership is a relationship. One of my colleagues at the Alban Institute, Richard Bass, uses the term "leaderism" for our culture's misplaced focus on the skills and traits of the solitary leader who will somehow see what others are missing and point to destinations others can't find. We mistakenly assume that leadership is based in the skills and activities of the individual person, so we try to build leaders rather than the right relationships through which leadership can be offered. Leadership resides not in the leader but in the "space between" the leader and the led. Leadership *is* relational.

Dan Smith's and Mary Sellon's work is important because they not only uncover the critical nature of relationship but offer ways to observe, connect, and change behaviors that are central to relational leadership. They observe that "pastors who possessed strong relational skills and worked at establishing healthy relationships thrived almost anywhere they went." I strongly agree. My experience, however, is that most of the excellent leaders I observe practice their art intuitively. Even the best leaders are hard pressed to explain what makes their leadership healthy and effective. Their inability to articulate what makes them good leaders demonstrates one of the reasons that leadership—as the saying goes—can be learned but not taught.

Smith and Sellon, however, provide a way for us to move from intuitive understanding to conscious awareness of leadership that enables us actually to make choices about our behavior as leaders. Using the foundational work of people like Daniel Goleman, John Gottman, Arnold and Amy Mindell, and others, Smith and Sellon undergird the ideal of right relationships by identifying the practices needed to build those relationships and develop as leaders ourselves. They offer us a map of relational leadership that shows us the ideas and issues we need to work with.

The authors rightly point to societal trends and technological advances that leave us even more isolated and detached from the relationships we seek and that God intends. I do believe, as Smith and Sellon state, that God created us to be in relationship. Nonetheless, we live in a culture that values individualism over relationship. The needs and preferences of the individual dominate; individuals see themselves as the final arbiters of what is good and true. This phenomenon has both a downside and an upside. In this environment, where "my truth" outweighs "our relationship," we should not be surprised that we have been experiencing a marked decrease in civility. Congregations can easily contribute to this cultural depression by over-focusing programs and attention on individuals' preferences and arguing about who is "right" rather than carefully discerning God's call to mission.

But like all good consultants, I believe that where there is a downside, there must also be an upside. I also believe we have the power to move toward the positive. The upside of an individualistic culture is that when people connect to a congregation, they truly expect that their faith will make a clear difference in their own lives. If I remember correctly, a report published sometime in the early 1970s indicated that the majority of Jews who were surveyed about what it meant to be a good Jew responded that it meant belonging to a synagogue with an observant rabbi—that is, a leader who expressed and practiced the faith. One can easily imagine Christians would have responded similarly. It was once enough to belong to a group that espoused certain values and practices. It was not necessary to express faith in one's own life or to practice behaviors that would distinguish one-self from others.

Today, however, individuals *do* want to be—and feel free to be—different, and they *do* want their faith to make a difference. The differences commonly have to do with their relationships. People want to feel their relationship with God, they want to explore and improve their relationships with their spouse or partner, their family, neighbors, and friends. People are now eager to explore their relationship to work, money, and possessions. This is clearly a moment when the question of right relationships is getting attention. Healthy, faithful leaders not only need to practice right relationships as a way of leading but must serve as models and mentors for others as they build right relationships in their own faith practice. Building right relationships goes even deeper than the question of how to lead and addresses the issue of how to live. Perhaps this is the greater purpose of leadership that we are expected to practice in congregations.

Gil Rendle

Preface

We invite you to join us in what has become the biggest adventure of our lives: learning about right relationships. We, Dan and Mary, are 65 and 45 years old, respectively. We've spent the majority of our lives in church settings where we heard about, studied, and preached on the concept of righteousness—being in right relationship with God, with neighbor, and with self. Yet we never really understood the practical implications of that for our daily relationships. Righteousness was an ethereal dream of how things should be, but rarely shaped our interactions as we sat around the table doing work with colleagues and team members. We were committed to the ideal of "love your neighbor," but at a loss for how to practice it in contentious meetings at the church. We didn't understand that our dream of righteousness could only be experienced to the extent that our daily interactions embodied right relationship.

About a decade ago we began to notice that some otherwise excellent programs failed to have impact. We watched seemingly insignificant or poorly planned events touch people in significant ways. People dropped out of churches that were vital and exciting. Other people stayed tenaciously loyal to churches that appeared to be ho-hum in the programs and facilities they offered. We noticed that some pastors flourished wherever they went. We saw that others with superior theological and practical training continually failed. What was it that made the difference?

What we discovered seemed so obvious and common-sensical, we hesitated to make much of it. Authentic, loving relationships repeatedly surfaced as the missing key element. The effectiveness and impact of a congregation's work, as well as the participant's sense of fulfillment and commitment, varied according to the quality of their relationships with each other. Pastors who possessed strong relational skills and worked at establishing healthy relationships thrived almost anywhere they went. Pastors less adept at relationships continually struggled even though they engaged in the same best practices as their colleagues.

The quality of relationships seemed to be the key. Relationships embodying qualities like caring, playfulness, collaboration, authenticity, and deep trust engendered commitment to God and personal fulfillment. They had a generative quality that fostered creativity and drew others in. These congregations' and committees' connection to God's Spirit was such that it didn't seem like they planned events as much as birthed them. These groups' paths were not always smooth; group members did not always agree. But, there was an energy, commitment, and audacity that other groups strove for, yet never attained.

We began to study everything we could find on relationships and how to do them well. We spent time with people from various disciplines and found that they were far ahead of much of the church in recognizing the transformational role of relationship. As is always the case, when the church forgets about a basic piece of the message with which it's been entrusted, that needed message bubbles up somewhere else. In the last five years the fields of business, education, psychology, and coaching have exploded with writings on the core importance of relationship. People in other fields had discovered what many faith communities had forgotten or dismissed as simplistic. Conscious and intentionally "right" relationships transform individuals and the systems of which they are a part.

In our ministry settings and our coaching and consulting practice we began to apply these concepts and skills of right relationship. The shifts required of us were challenging and at times scary. The impact on us and on others was dramatic. The word *transformational* appropriately describes the shift in our own lives and in life within the groups we led.

We've discovered, as have many others, that the skills for right relationship can be learned. Practical skills in self-awareness, self-management, social awareness, and relationship management are all needed. Through daring to practice, both skill and confidence can be built.

This book brings together the work of researchers and practitioners from a variety of disciplines. Daniel Goleman's work in emotional intelligence is foundational, as are John Gottman's discoveries about what prompts relationships (his work primarily focuses on marriages) to succeed or fail. Arnold and Amy Mindell's work in the field of process psychology offers new insights on how to understand what's trying to happen in and through our relationships. Faith Fuller and Marita Fridjhon are the founders of the Center for Right Relationship. Their practical methods for creating, sustaining, and empowering meaningful relationships have been invaluable to us and our work.

How This Book Is Organized

In this book, we've taken what we have learned and continue to learn and distilled it down to a basic how-to of theory, story, and exercises. Think of it as a learning lab designed to help you and your group reflect, experience, and build the skills that make relationships lively and life-giving. Relationships happen so fast that they seem to be automatic; we meet someone and things just happen. Actually, every relationship is constructed through a series of moments where choices are made. For the sake of learning and building skills, we deconstruct relational exchanges into some basic building blocks. Each chapter will cover a different and necessary component of creating conscious and intentional relationships.

Our hope is that it will help you, and in turn your congregation, build and maintain the loving relationships that provide the medium for God's transforming work.

How to Use This Book

The introduction to this book lays out our understanding of right relationship: our longing for it and God's intent for us to live that way. The next five chapters focus on developing the skills for forming and living right relationships.

- Chapter 1 addresses self-awareness. Skills for developing awareness of where we are, what we feel, what we value, and what we dream are covered in this chapter.
- Chapter 2 focuses on managing our feelings and perspectives by utilizing choice and commitment.
- Chapter 3 looks at developing awareness of the people around us. This chapter offers ways to get to know someone in deeper than normal ways.
- Chapter 4 puts together the preceding skills and offers six essential questions and choices to help us love another person.
- Chapter 5 takes us into forming and living right relationships.
- Chapter 6, "Troubleshooting: Questions and Answers," responds to real-life situations as people apply the principles and skills found in the book.

Use this book with the groups you work with. Follow it chapter by chapter, for each chapter builds on the prior one. Take some time in each meeting to move through a chapter or part of a chapter. This work may take what you consider valuable time from your planned agenda. We encourage you to set aside time for it and see what happens. Our experience is that working with this material results in both more satisfying relationships and increased effectiveness.

Practice the ideas and skills in all of your relationships. The concepts and exercises in this book are just as helpful to groups of two people (partners, couples, staff pairs, cochairs) as they are to larger teams or committees. We encourage you to keep a journal and record your experiences along the way. The act of writing our learnings down helps anchor them.

We invite you to stand in the place of curiosity as you move through the chapters of the book. Curiosity about yourself, about the person sitting next to you. Curiosity about what new and even scary thing might happen next. God is with you. May your adventure into right relationship be transformational for you and for all those around you.

Introduction | # The Importance of Right Relationship

A s they did every year, almost 200 of the Methodist clergy of the region gathered for the purpose of tending to their collegial relationships with each other. Many had known and worked with each other for over 30 years. The annual retreat afforded the opportunity to connect with old friends as well as make new ones. Brian arrived, as did the majority of the others this year, with an anxious stomach. The social issues that divided their denomination divided the clergy. Distrust ran high and long-time colleagues threatened schism. The annual gathering had grown increasingly contentious over the past four years. Anticipating an even further escalation over recent events, nearly 100 clergy simply chose not to attend this year.

Those who came arrived with little hope. Brian, a younger pastor, had already decided that he would keep his head down and stay out of the line of fire as much as possible. As the group filled the meeting room for their initial time together, people were quiet and wary. Worship began their time together. Brian found singing familiar hymns and songs was pleasant, but noticed that his and other voices were subdued as if no one was truly connecting to the music and its message.

The preacher of the day was a pastor from that region. She recalled the words of the apostle Paul as he wrote about being with the community in Rome. "I am longing to see you," he wrote (Rom. 1:11a). The preacher paused and then confessed, "Unlike Paul, as I thought about this gathering, I was not longing to be here with you." She shared what it had been like for her these past years as the community grew more fractured. Her dream of collegial community slipped away a bit more each time they met.

"The problem," she continued, "is I know you all. I know all about you. I've arrived knowing squarely in my mind what you each stand for and how you will treat me and how you cannot be trusted." The room fell silent and she continued. "The problem is that I know you so well, that I no longer see you. I need to learn to see you

Until we stop simply knowing each other, and start seeing each other, things will not change.

again fresh in this moment, a child of God, gifted and graced and placed here for a purpose. And, I need to let you see who I am. What frightens me, what exhilarates me, what my heart longs for. Until we stop simply knowing each other, and start seeing each other, things will not change."

As she preached, the mood in the room softened and heads nodded. That softening continued into the prayer time that followed and the closing hymns rang with renewed power. The new mood was short lived. Following worship, the retreat leader announced that during the night they had assigned the clergy to small groups. Though people had indicated their willingness to participate as they registered, backs stiffened and the temperature in the room dropped several degrees. Brian wondered if it was too late to back out of participating in a small group.

The names of the people comprising the first group were read and anxiety intensified. The leadership had placed together in one group the eight most vocal and volatile people on either side of the divisive issues. Brian swallowed hard; would anybody be left alive at the end of this? As he heard the names for his group announced, he felt his shoulders relax a tiny bit. "I don't agree with all of them," he thought, "but I can at least sit with them. I just won't say anything."

Brian and the other members of his small group pulled their chairs into a circle. While some of the groups found other rooms to meet in, his group and six others stayed in the large gathering space. Brian looked around the room at the other groups. People seemed wary and tense. Turning back to his own group, he saw the same thing.

Each group had been given an outline they could follow. Brian's group agreed to the suggested covenant agreements: holding confidentiality, listening to and respecting each participant, and nurturing an open heart and mind. "What's not there that we'd like to add?" someone asked. A long silence ensued as people looked at the paper or down at the carpet. Belinda finally blurted, "This isn't really an addition to the ground rules. But as I look at what they want us to talk about, it would really help me if I understood your theology. Who do you understand God to be and how do you think God works?" Brian blinked hard along with everyone else. That question got right to the meat of things. He looked at Belinda and saw that she really seemed curious. Knowing he was taking a risk and that his spontaneous comments might draw the disdain or disapproval of others, he plunged in. "You mean like . . ." and off he went.

At first as he shared, he stared at the floor, scared to see how the other members of the group might be responding to his words. When he glanced up, he was surprised to see the softness in their faces and their encouraging nods. Each person took a turn, the others asking questions to better understand. As the sharing progressed, Brian noticed how different he felt: curious and energized. He noticed how fond he was of these people, how tender he felt towards them.

As their time drew to a close, someone asked, "What just happened here between us? It feels so different now." Another commented, "I think we let go of knowing things about each other, and started seeing each other." The group nodded. They closed with prayer and promised to gather again for the afternoon small-group time.

Brian showed up to the afternoon session with high hopes. The morning had gone so well. The group started up again, but it soon became clear that whatever warmth and tenderness had been there in the morning, was not there now. A self-conscious wariness pervaded the group. They went through their time together but something was missing. Only at the end did someone mention the change in the group from their morning session, "We're different this afternoon." "Yes," added another, "it feels like we're on guard." The group took the last 10 minutes to talk about the shift. George summed it up when he said, "We create something new every time we come together. This morning we created one way of being with each other; this afternoon we created something else. How we are with each other and the nature of our relationship is in our hands."

We determine the nature of our relationships.

We Hunger for Relationship

Without relationship, we perish. Without loving relationships, we rarely thrive. We long for our relationships to be positive. We want them to connect us with other people in creative and life-giving ways. We feel a sense of appreciative awe when we truly "see" someone . . . and are seen by them. Positive relationships support and nurture us. They connect us, letting us know we're not alone. They sustain us in difficult times and add pleasure to our celebrations.

Part of what draws people to faith communities is their desire for caring and supportive relationships. A recent Sunday morning discussion at a Presbyterian church focused on why people chose to be part of that congregation. "I'm allowed to speak my mind here and so can others. And even when we disagree, we listen," said one woman, "and people respect me." An older man said, "This congregation is my family. People greet me by name and are genuinely glad to see me." "I'm doing things in my life I never thought I could do. And it's because of the encouragement and support I receive here," contributed a single mother. To a person, their comments lifted up the importance of relationship.

Establishing meaningful relationships is of primary importance to congregants. One might assume then that Judeo-

Christian faith communities with their emphasis on covenantal relationship would be relationship experts. Frequently, this is not the case. After many years away, Harold and his family began attending a faith community again. By day he directed facilities development for a large medical cooperative. A year later after taking membership vows, he was asked to share his expertise and oversee property matters for the congregation. Knowing his busy schedule, he hesitated. But the pastor was persuasive about their need of him and so Harold agreed. Before long, the woman's guild recruited his wife to help with the annual rummage sale and the nursery enlisted their daughter to babysit.

The pastor received a letter from Harold one Tuesday morning, explaining why he and his family had not been in worship the previous week. As they had climbed into the car that morning, they'd allowed themselves to ask out loud the unthinkable question: "Why are we doing this?"

Their faith community had become a continuation of the busy and impersonal life they lived the other six days of the week. Much was demanded from them simply for the maintenance of the religious institution. The relationships, though polite and pleasant, were no different than those in the workplace. The inquiry, "How are you?" was asked with the same expectation of a surface response. They longed for a place where they could move beyond the surface, where they could safely share their hopes and fears, where they would be challenged to explore new aspects of themselves and the world. They longed for right relationship.

People are often initially drawn to a faith community because it offers programs or features that meet situational needs in their lives; however, studies reveal that if people do not form a significant relational connection within the first six weeks, they drift away. Some may

> *People long for meaningful relationships. Strong programs and lovely facilities are not enough.*

stay for the sake of the children or for the duration of a crisis. But then, if their deeper need for intimacy has not been met, they disappear.

Facilities and programs, no matter how excellent, do not finally satisfy unless the deeper relational needs are met. A marvelous facility with an outstanding staff and top-of-the-line equipment may initially draw a person but is not finally what holds them and transforms them.

God's Intent for Us

God created us to be in relationship. Our earliest stories tell of God's desires for us. In the story of Adam and Eve, God recognizes the deep need of the human heart for connection and community. God gives Eve to Adam as a partner, saying, "It is good that the man should not be alone" (Gen. 2:18a). God intends our relationships to be not only fulfilling, but generative. God's command to "be fruitful" (Gen. 1:28) applies to all of our relationships. Work teams and staff partnerships, no less than marriages, are intended to be creative relationships, birthing new ideas and projects that further God's work in the world.

> *God intends for our relationships to be effective, fulfilling, and generative.*

Though God intends fulfilling and creative relationships for us, we often make choices that take us and the world to a different place. Our scriptures are filled with stories of failed relationships. Cain farmed. Abel raised sheep. Each young man had his own path in life. Life went smoothly until jealousy crept into their relationship. We can imagine that it was a dark and sad day for God as the intended mutuality degenerated into deep separation. Distance grew as comparison and self-doubt filled Cain, until he could no longer stand the sight of his brother. Finally, Cain lured his brother Abel out into a field, where he killed him.

The same separation and even destructiveness repeatedly manifests itself on a world scale and even in faith communities. Jorene was the young and warm associate pastor of St. Matthew's Church. She loved her work there, but found her relationship with her senior pastor deteriorating. The senior pastor, jealous of how people responded to Jorene, took every opportunity to subtly but publicly put her in her place. The demeaning comments grew in frequency and intensity until finally, for her sake and the sake of the church, Jorene resigned. Bruised and broken, Jorene did not go back into another church for a year and a half.

God wants far more for us, our faith communities, and for the world. The deep longings of God find expression through the prophets. Through them, we hear God's dreams of the day when people and nations "shall beat their swords into plowshares, and their spears into pruning hooks; nation shall not

Right relationship refers to being in the proper or God-intended position in relationship to others.

lift up sword against nation, neither shall they learn war any more" (Isa. 2:4; Mic. 4:3). God longs for us to be in right relationship with each other.

By "right" we don't mean "right and wrong." The word in this context refers to being in an appropriate, healthy, or God-intended position in relationship to others. In God's vision for creation, people relate to each other in particular ways. These relationships are characterized by honor, respect, love, and care. Right relationships are creative, mutual, and generative; life-giving things are birthed. When we are in right relationship we embody these God-intended ways of being with each other. Righting a tipped-over vase restores its functional-

Right relationships are honoring, respectful, loving, caring, mutual, and generative.

ity. Righting our relationships restores the fullness of their functionality as well.

The swords may not be visible as teams and committees gather for their work, but the absence of right relationships just as effectively separates and divides people. A façade of love and the exterior trappings of civility are not enough. Without true honoring, caring, and being open to and welcoming what God is birthing through us together, God's dream for creation remains unfulfilled. Carter Heyward suggests, "I suppose nothing is more heartbreaking to God herself than the denial of our power to recognize, call forth, and celebrate right relation among ourselves."[1] The state of all things living in right relationship is summed up in the Hebrew word *shalom*. Shalom refers not just to the cessation of war, but to a state of active and creative peace that brings life and joy. God's dream is for shalom to be experienced here on earth—now.

Another image of right relationship lived out, is the "kindom" of God. In the kindom, all people are brothers and sisters. All people are children of God. All people have different gifts and purposes, but are of equal worth. Strangers are family members we simply have not met yet. In the kindom, all of life is interrelated. Effectiveness and fulfillment are experienced by individuals only to the extent that they are experienced by the total family, and vice versa. Thinking about God's creation as a kindom reminds us of the centrality of our developing caring and generative relationships.

In the kindom, all of life is interrelated. Effectiveness and fulfillment are experienced by individuals only to the extent that they are experienced by the total family, and vice versa.

The Problem

Although the scriptures and our faith traditions lift up the centrality of relationship, we often form and tend to our relationships haphazardly. It's tempting to think that we are autonomous, the captains of our own souls. The truth is that our lives are a web of relationships. Almost every aspect of our lives depends on, flows from, or influences someone else. If we are to live the creative and fulfilling lives God intends for us, our relational web must in good working order.

Our relational skills, however, have decreased rapidly across the past decades. Societal trends coupled with technological advances have left us even more isolated and unable to create and maintain long-term covenantal relationships. Today's divorce rate indicates the difficulty people have in maintaining sustainable, loving relationships. It also indicates that the nuclear family currently provides an unpredictable crucible for developing the relational skills needed for such relationships. With one of the primary training grounds for developing relational skills eroded, faith communities have a unique opportunity to serve society. Their theological understanding and missional focus uniquely positions them to help people develop strong and healthy relationships with spouses, children, coworkers, and neighbors.

For many congregations, living out love is an intellectually affirmed, "Why, of course" value, but not a lived core value. Congregations say, "Why, of course we love God. Why, of course we love our neighbors. Why, of course we love each other." We don't doubt that they do. But at the same time, inventories of congregation members and their neighborhoods reveal congregations often are unable to live out that love in daily, concrete, felt ways. Most materials assume that congregations know how to "do" relationships. That is not our experience.

> *For many congregations, living out love is an intellectually affirmed, "Why, of course" value, but not a lived core value.*

We believe that people do not lack the desire for stepping more deeply into right relationship. People want to love and be loved. They long for satisfying and creative relationships. What stands in people's way is knowing how to create and maintain right relationships. As we stand alongside congregations and congregational leaders we find them eager to engage in ministry practices that will help them live out their purpose more effectively. We also find them ignoring the very thing that would help them do that. Only through developing right relationships will they be fully available for the work God wants to accomplish through them in the world. This book intends to help people explore and live out conscious and intentional loving relationships—what we call "right relationships." It is through right relationship that individuals find transformation and fulfillment and congregations realize their missional purpose.

We have discovered, as have many others, that good relational skills can be learned and honed across time. Practical skills in self-awareness, self-management, social awareness, and relationship management are all needed. Through practice, these skills can be built, confidence developed, and right relationship lived.

> *Good relational skills can be learned and honed across time.*

Learning to Form and Live Right Relationships

Russell held responsibility for the oversight, well-being, and development of pastors, lay leadership, and congregations in his geographical area. He and seven other judicatory leaders formed the leadership team that guided the life of over 300 congregations. Committed to furthering the greater mission of the religious community, Russell stayed current with the latest writings in the area of management and leadership. He believed with certainty that he was wiser and smarter than his colleagues. Masterful at subtle manipulation, group decisions almost always reflected Russell's desires. People and congregations benefited enough from his knowledge and insights to reinforce in Russell's mind that his approach with colleagues was warranted.

Over time, the effects of Russell's way of relating with other members of the leadership team began manifesting themselves. The others began behaving toward him as he had acted toward them. E-mails were sent that he was not copied on. Leadership team members would meet together prior to gatherings of the large group to strategize how to work around him. People treated him with suspicion and hostility. Russell found himself feeling more and more marginalized as well as less able to achieve the missional ends that were so important to him. His unwillingness and inability to work openly and collaboratively with his colleagues was hurting him, them, and the religious community he loved so much.

Russell decided the time had come to learn to do things differently. He turned his learning focus to relationships. He read everything he could get his hands on and attended any workshop or training that seemed pertinent. Slowly, over the space of several years, Russell changed the way he interacted with people. Abandoning his arrogance, he began recognizing the gifts inherent even in the simplest and least-honored people. He became curious about people and started listening for the wisdom they might have. He stopped "selling" and started sharing with others his honest thoughts and feelings.

People who had not known Russell before found him warm and authentic. His colleagues on the leadership team, however, did not know what to think. Having experienced the old Russell for so many years, they were not sure this new one could be trusted. Perhaps it was just another ruse, another manipulation. This saddened Russell, demonstrating even more fully how his way of relating to them had affected the entire group. He realized that through the way he had related to people he had helped create a monster that now had a life of its own.

Russell no longer enjoyed that environment, but having helped create it, he could not walk away. Still committed to the mission, he knew he must remain, and that together they could transform that monster into a taste of God's kindom. That would be the most effective way he could help move the religious community he loved towards fulfilling its mission.

Life-giving relationships happen neither automatically nor magically. They are created by people who make the choice to be open, authentic, caring, and curious with each other. The skills required to create and maintain such relationships can be learned. Right relationships are important not only for the fulfillment they bring each participant, but also for what gets created through them.

> *Making the choice to be open, authentic, caring, and curious with each other creates life-giving relationships.*

These relationships are a vehicle through which God works and effects change in the world. The stronger and healthier our relationships, the clearer channels they can be for what God wants to birth in the world.

Choice: A Fundamental Affirmation

The journey into right relationship takes work and courage. It would be far easier to just continue living together in the patterns that have become natural for us. The compelling reason for the journey is the value of the goal before us—the kindom of God and what that means for us, for our congregations, and for the world. The reality? Right relationships are messy. They require intentional, deliberate work that will be uncomfortable at times. They demand that we learn new skills and practice them. But these skills can be learned. The difference they make for us as individuals, for the greater systems we are a part of, and for the world makes it worth every ounce of effort.

Note

1.   Carter Heyward, *Touching Our Strength: The Erotic as Power and Love of God* (San Francisco: HarperSanFrancisco, 1989), 21.

Chapter
One | # Developing Self-Awareness

*R*ight relationships help people feel honored and challenged, supported and held accountable. As people experience right relationship they experience the kindom of God. Their very best is called out from them both as individuals and as a group in the relational container of love and care. And though right relationships may look as easy as a Fred Astaire and Ginger Rogers dance number, right relationships are far more complex. Not only do they require multiple skills simultaneously, relationships are also improvisational interactions, created and danced in the moment. Life-giving and generative relationships require competence in relational skills and the ability to use those skills creatively in the moment.

Self-Awareness: The First of Four Basic Skill Areas

Daniel Goleman's research reveals basic building blocks for good relationships. His field of research, called emotional intelligence, provides insight into the basic skill areas that impact relationships and thus the productivity of teams and individuals. Goleman's work reveals that technical knowledge and education are not enough for superior job performance. Positive, healthy relationships with peers and the public is the additional factor that marks the highly effective worker.

Goleman outlines four basic areas in which skills must be developed in order for a person to create and maintain good relationships: self-awareness, self-management, social awareness, and relational management. Research in business settings reveals that when teams and their leaders do not master competencies in these four areas, relationships flounder and productivity suffers. This holds true for faith communities as well.

The four basic skill areas for developing good relationships are:
1. Self-awareness
2. Self-management
3. Social awareness
4. Relational management

We use Goleman's four skill areas as a way of breaking down the complex process of relational interaction into manageable chunks. In each of these four areas we identify helpful competencies in the chapters that follow: some of them surfaced by Goleman, some surfaced by other researchers, and some surfaced through our work with pastors and congregations. The skill areas progressively build on each other. Self-awareness provides the foundational building block.

What We Mean by Self-Awareness

Right relationship does not begin with the relationship, or even the other person with whom we want to have that relationship; it begins with us. Are we awake to where we are and what is going on around us? Are we aware of our attitudes and feelings, and the deeper values, hopes, and fears that give rise to them? The foundational skill for developing and maintaining right relationships is self-awareness. Self-awareness in basic terms means being present in the moment to what we are feeling and what's important to us.

Self-awareness: being present in the moment to what we are feeling and what's important to us

We walk into a meeting thinking about the fight brewing at home. During the discussion, a new member makes an offhand remark and we take him to task with a vehemence that surprises us . . . and everybody else. Where did that come from? Or, perhaps our mind has already jumped ahead to picking up the kids after band practice and we're fretting about whether we'll get there on time. Every time someone asks a question or makes a comment that slows things down we sigh deeply and roll our eyes in frustration. The meeting proceeds as ponderously as we had feared.

It is a common occurrence. Our body sits in the chair, but our mind and our heart drift somewhere else—pondering over the past or preparing for the future. And when our mind and heart are not present, we are not fully present as a participant in the group.

Jon's day at work had been horrid. Sitting in the finance committee meeting that evening, he kept rerunning in his head the presentation he had made and what he could have done differently. Jon wondered what his colleagues and supervisor at work were thinking and he worried about his reputation. Jon left the finance meeting an hour and a half later without much awareness of what had happened there or much awareness of his preoccupation. He felt the committee meeting had been lifeless and dragged on without realizing that his own preoccupation had contributed to that experience.

"Know thyself" is as wise an injunction today as when Socrates spoke it and is foundational to healthy and productive relationships. Know where you are, what you feel, what you value, and what you dream. This provides the flexibility and freedom to interact consciously, intentionally, and creatively with other people. Self-awareness increases our capacity to experience our own lives.

Foundational to self-awareness:
- *Know where you are*
- *Know what you feel*
- *Know what you value*
- *Know what you dream*

Self-awareness involves development in four areas. The first, awareness of where we are, refers to knowing where we are in time and space and being awake to the present moment. Not in the past or in the future, but in the *now*. Aware of where we are, we know what actually surrounds us in our environment and the circumstances we face. The second area is awareness of what we're feeling. Awareness of our feelings (and how we feel about having them) allows us to back up a bit from the experience of the emotion itself. That distance permits choice about how we will express our feelings. The third, awareness of what we value, allows us to be true to ourselves and authentic with others. Knowing what we value helps us decide where to put our time and energy. The fourth, awareness of what we dream, connects us with our hopes and fears and God's deepest longings for us. We know better what vision we want to give ourselves to embody. Developing competencies in these four areas is the first step toward building relationships with others that are loving, generative, and life giving.

Knowing Where You Are

Ginger did it just the other day with Sam—she was there, but not there. Discussing an upcoming project on the telephone, Ginger heard the chime indicating new e-mail had arrived in her inbox. As Sam continued to speak, Ginger made all the appropriate noises, "uh-huh . . . sure . . . go on," while she proceeded to open and read her mail. The line grew quiet. "What are you doing? Reading your e-mail?" Sam asked. Busted. Miles away with no visible cues, Sam could tell Ginger was not present.

Ginger's not being present had several effects on Sam. He immediately felt unimportant, like he was wasting her time. That led to a flash of irritation. Things were rectified easily, but Sam was a bit less confident and at ease for the rest of the conversation.

We think we are hiding it—smiling and nodding our head, looking the person directly in the eye—yet there's nothing behind our own eyes except a blank wall. What our eyes are seeing is not getting through to our deeper being nor is our deeper being engaging with what's being seen. In those instances, we kid no one but ourselves. Others can tell when we're not present, even though we think we are hiding it expertly.

So much of life gets lived this way—either remembering and replaying events from the past or rehearsing things for the future. Rarely do we live in the present, the now, this very moment. Sometimes we find ourselves living, not in the past or the future, but in a parallel present. When we multitask, daydream, or talk compulsively, we become lost in our own private worlds and disconnect from others. Our preoccupation impacts other people. But the person who is hurt the most, the person who is cheated the most, is ourself. Life is not lived in the past; the past is only a memory. Life is lived in the present. Not in the past; not in the future; only in the now. Nor do we live in the future; the future can only be imagined. The only place where we are alive and breathing and capable of living in real and interactive ways, the only place where we can meet God, or anyone else, is now—the present moment that we are in. Life is lived in the present.

> *Life is lived in the present. Not in the past; not in the future; only in the now.*

The importance of being present has long been recognized by faith communities and practiced in a variety of ways, both corporate and personal. An invocation invites people to bring their minds and hearts into the present moment even as it invokes God's presence. A call to worship reminds people where they are and why they're there, calling them to the experience right there before them. The personal discipline of meditation is not an escape from the present moment, but a deep and exquisite noticing of it.

Exercise 1.1

Experiencing the Now

Being in the now is basic to self-awareness. The first exercise will help you shift from the past or future and into the present moment. Short and simple, it can be done anywhere anytime you need a bit of "awakening" to where you are. Do it four times a day for a week and see what you notice. You will need a journal for this exercise.

Take a deep breath and become aware of what your senses perceive about your environment at this very moment. Without judging them or attaching meaning to them, simply note the following in your head:

- Four things you see
- Four things you hear
- Four things you smell
- Four things your skin perceives through touch
- Four things you taste

After you finish, take a quick inventory of your thoughts, your emotional state, and what your body is feeling. Note in your journal what has shifted for you.

Imagine a meeting of eight people where eight bodies are sitting around a table and all eight minds are somewhere else. That describes the first 45 minutes of a recent meeting. The first segment of the meeting was frustrating and unproductive. Forty-five minutes into the meeting Elaine said, "Where are we today? We all seem a million miles away." The team members realized none of them were very present and they weren't getting anything done. Elaine's comment helped them let go of their preoccupations and shifted the tenor of the meeting considerably.

Simple rituals or exercises at the beginning of meetings help group members become conscious of attitudes or leftover business they've brought into the meeting with them. Think of these rituals not as opening devotions, but ways to encourage people to make an intentional transition into the group and its work. One committee, at the beginning of its meetings, passes around a cardboard box. People name and place into the box things from their day they don't want to bring into that night's meeting. The box and its contents are committed to God's care and placed next to the door, where people can pick them up (if they wish) after the meeting ends. Another chair makes a habit of asking committee members, "As we begin tonight, what do you need to say or do or let go of to help you be fully here?"[1]

Knowing What You Feel

At any given moment we are a complex collection of emotions, biases, desires, and passions, many of which are unknown to our conscious selves. When we are unaware of the feelings that we feel, we run the risk of being controlled by them.

The leadership team Martin served on was attempting to move to a deeper level of caring and authenticity with each other. Martin had a less than positive history with several key members of the team. There had been times in the past when he had felt mistreated, even abused by those individuals. In the past year, his relationship with them had improved tremendously, but that afternoon's invitation to be open with each other unleashed a torrent of feelings he didn't know he still had. Martin was unaware of the depth of those feelings—anger, resentment, guilt, defensiveness, the longing for acceptance—and thus unprepared and unable to manage them as they poured out. The group, still taking baby steps toward intimacy, did not yet have the skills to know what to do with Martin's outburst. The group found their way back eventually, but the team regressed several steps that day in its ability to function effectively.

Martin came to see that day as a gift, albeit a painful one, convincing him of the importance of developing greater self-awareness. If we do not learn to manage our feelings, they manage us. And managing feelings is impossible unless first we know that we have them.

> *If we don't manage our feelings, they manage us.*

Our feelings come from many places; they can arise from remembered experiences in the past. Sometimes what we're feeling is more closely linked with those past experiences than what's happening to us in the present moment. In such instances, feelings bubble up when something or someone around us reminds us of that past event. If we are unaware of what is happening, we can confuse the two experiences and react to the present one as though it were the past event. Every time Steve stands up from the meeting table and leans against the back wall, Jaime feels resentment rising. Jaime remembers a former colleague who did a similar thing. He is convinced Steve is trying to take command of the group like his former colleague did. In reality, Steve simply has a bad back and cannot sit comfortably for long stretches.

Feelings can also indicate that an area of deep importance to us is being touched on. A flash of joy during a meeting may indicate that we are sensing the group take a step toward a long-held hope. A spark of panic may be a clue that something important is about to be lost. Feelings can indicate a variety of things, but until we notice and name the feelings we have, it's almost impossible to understand the message they carry. The trick then is noticing and naming feelings as they course through us.

Knowing what we're feeling is not always easy. Not all people are adept in the world of emotions. Asked how they're feeling in a difficult moment, many might be able to say, "uncomfortable," but not be able to label that feeling any more precisely than that. Some might not even be able to identify that much. "How am I feeling? I don't know. Okay, I guess." People have different levels of awareness and comfort when it comes to emotions. And, we have different levels of awareness at different times. Sometimes we get so caught up in what we are doing or even in what we are feeling that we fail to notice that we are feeling anything.

Though often overlooked, our own bodies can provide physical indicators or signals that we're feeling something. These signals from our body point us toward information about those feelings. A signal is a physical indicator that something is happening emotionally. Feelings are invisible, but their impact is not. Feelings affect us on a physical sensory level. Irritation at the slowness of the grocery line has us tapping our fingers on the cart. Indecision over a choice has us shifting our weight from foot to foot. The tone of our voice and the movements of our body shift as our feelings shift.

Jingling a coin may be a signal that we're feeling impatient. Butterflies in our stomach may signal nervousness. Melissa knows that when her hand goes to her throat it's often a signal that she's feeling overwhelmed. Signals can be visual (my eye keeps going back to that picture of the waterfall) or auditory (I keep making this little sigh) or movement based (I keep scratching my head) or bodily sensations (the hair on my arms rises; my stomach churns).

For many people, signals offer a path to knowing what they are feeling. The meaning of signals varies from person to person and from instance to instance. Drumming fingers may signal impatience, worry, excitement, or a hundred other things, or nothing at all. The thing to do with a signal is notice it and get curious about what feeling or experience it might point to. "Hmmm. I notice that I keep looking out the window. I wonder what that's about? I know I'd much rather be out there than in here. I just realized

> *Noticing our gestures, our tone of voice, and our body sensations provides clues to what we're feeling.*

this meeting is getting very tense and I am too." Here the visual signal of the alluring window offered the first sign of growing tension within the person.

The first exercise in this chapter helped awaken you to experience the moment called now. This next exercise helps build awareness of what you're feeling in a given moment. Awareness is the fundamental first step in learning to be in control of your feelings rather than being controlled by them.

Exercise 1.2

How Are You?

Try this exercise over the course of the next week in various settings. You may find it helpful to do the exercise in written form in your journal each time, or to work it through in your head and record it in your journal later. If you are working through this book with a small group, share your experiences with each other at your next group meeting.

- Without judging or looking for meaning, simply notice the following:
- What is on your mind?
- Notice whether your mind is focusing on something in the past, in the future, or in the present.
- Notice whether your mind is focusing on something related to the task at hand, or not at all.

- What are you aware of in your body? (Tenseness in your neck? Knots in your stomach? A swinging foot?)
- What in your environment captures your attention? (A sound? A sight? A smell?)
- What is your dominant feeling at this moment? (Joyful, excited, engaged, peaceful, tender, afraid, annoyed, angry, pained, sad, bored, confused, impatient, curious?)
- What is the feeling of [see above list] about?

Knowing What You Value

Awareness of our feelings provides a window into those things that we hold most dear: our values and our dreams. When an editorial enrages us, it has touched on something deeply important to us. A news story that is interesting but fails to move us emotionally engages our head but not our heart. When we react with significant feeling, we know that something we value is being touched on.

Our feelings provide a window into our values and dreams.

Values are the principles and standards for living that are foundationally important to us. Values form our intrinsic inner Geiger counter. When we act in ways that honor our personal values, we feel fulfillment and a sense of aliveness—a sense of being true to ourselves. When we act in ways that are counter to our values—or when we are in encounters that discount our values—we feel frustrated, angry or deadened, as if we are selling out or being dishonored.

Values: *foundationally important principles and standards*

For example, if we value "homemade hospitality," we'll feel alive and true to ourselves when we create welcoming space for others that is warm and personal. We'll appreciate it when someone sends us a handmade card or invites us to share freshly made chicken soup and freshly baked bread. If we value "colorful creativity," working in an environment that demands subdued uniformity will leave us feeling as if we cannot breathe. A value of authenticity leads us to long for places of openness and honesty; deception drives us crazy.

Values honored leave us feeling fulfilled and alive. Values stepped on or ignored leave us feeling constrained and frustrated. No two people share the exact same set of values. And that's where things get interesting. Take the case of Cathy and Rob. Cathy really values homemade hospitality; for her a handmade card says love and care. Rob really values professional excellence. The first year they served together as cochairs of the welcoming committee, they nearly came to blows. Cathy wanted to organize a group of people who would bake cookies for newcomers. Rob

> *Values honored leave us feeling fulfilled and alive. Values stepped on or ignored leave us feeling constrained and frustrated.*

felt strongly that while a welcoming gift was important, homemade cookies sent the wrong image and could be a health concern. He pushed for plastic water bottles with the congregation's name printed on them and a brochure tucked inside. Cathy was aghast at such a cold and impersonal approach.

Every time a project came up, Rob and Cathy butted heads until both of them began to think about stepping down from the committee. It took them several months to figure out what was going on. Once they did, other mysterious conflicts from the past made sense. It was Rob who discovered it first. Conversation grew heated as they discussed a new brochure. While Cathy wanted the members of the committee to produce it, Rob felt the brochure should be designed by a professional.

"I just realized something," Rob interjected. "My family didn't have a lot of money growing up and store-bought things were rare. Somewhere along the line I came to believe that store-bought, professionally made things were better and giving them to someone said you truly valued that person." The argument stopped. Cathy looked at him as if seeing him for the first time and said, "I'm just the opposite. Both my parents worked. Dinner was either takeout or prepared from a box. Birthday cakes came from the bakery. I grew up wishing that someone would care enough to take the time to make things from scratch for me."

That little moment of self-awareness on each other's part provided insight into an ongoing struggle that had seemed unresolvable. When what we value is dismissed as unimportant, it can feel like we are being dismissed as unimportant. Though our values may shift some over time, values are not chosen. They are an essential part of who we are and arise from our personality, our upbringing, and our experiences. Having lived with them so long, we may not be aware of them. Or, being so used to them ourselves, we may think that everyone thinks the same way.

Exercise 1.3

Looking for Values

The goal for this exercise is to end up with a list of four to six values that are important to you. Record your reflections in your journal. If you are working through this book with a group, share your reflections at your next gathering.

1. Recall a moment when life seemed perfect. What was going on that contributed to that perfect feeling?

   - What was the setting?
   - Who were you with?
   - What were you doing?
   - What values were being honored at that moment?

2. What annoys you or drives you crazy? What values are being stepped on when that happens?

3. What do you get obsessive about? (This can be an indicator of a value taken to the extreme.) What value is at the root of what you get obsessive about?

Knowing What You Dream

What we long for and what we dread shapes us. The way we dream about the future influences our thoughts, feelings, and

actions. The field of process psychology differentiates between two kinds of dreams: high dreams (our best hopes)
and low dreams (our worst fears). High dreams reflect our
greatest hopes and deepest desires both for the long term
and for the situation immediately in front of us. Low dreams
reveal our deepest fears and in-
securities about what will happen. Both high dreams and low
dreams are always present,
though at any given moment one

High dreams reflect our greatest hopes and deepest desires. Low dreams reveal our deepest fears and insecurities.

typically dominates our thoughts, feelings, and behaviors
more than the other. The environment we are in, the events
and people around us, and our own attitude and state of
health support us being closer to either our high dream for
the situation we are in or our low dream.

When we live closer to our high dreams, we speak and
act in accordance with our best hopes, our words and actions already beginning to embody that longed-for state. When
our low dream dominates us, our feelings, words, and actions
begin to reflect that dreaded place. Contrary to what one
might think, high dreams are not good, nor low dreams bad.
Each serves in its own way. High dreams lure us ahead. Low
dreams alert us to the things we do not want to create unwittingly. They sound a warning signal. We create from our
dreams, therefore we must know what we're dreaming.

The first chapters of this book were due in two days. We
were on a tight writing schedule, exchanging what we had
written at the end of each day. Mary's father had died four
weeks prior and she had traveled back to the Midwest to
take care of her father's estate. She wrote early in the morn-
ings and late at night and did all the things that needed to be
done to settle her father's affairs in between. It was a lot to
do, but she was committed to meeting the deadline. Not wanting to let either Dan or her family down, she tried to project
confidence that everything could be accomplished in a timely
manner. She became more brittle, however, by the minute.

By 11 P.M. on Sunday night she couldn't write another
word. As she got ready to send her work to Dan, she realized

how scared she was for him to read it, how poorly she thought she was holding up her end of the project. Even worse, she questioned the value and viability of the work. Living closer to her low dream, her worst fears ran rampant. The deadline would be missed, the book project would be dropped, and her friendship with Dan would fall apart.

It was her fingernail constantly tapping the edge of her mug that night which alerted her. "What's that about?" she wondered. "I'm nervous," she realized, "nervous about sending this to Dan. Worried that he's going to tell me I'm not working hard enough and should drop out of the project. I feel like giving up." She wrote that in an e-mail to him that night, adding, "Here's today's work. I'm really feeling discouraged and fearful. If you can do it, I need you to be a cheerleader for me."

It hadn't dawned on Mary to share her fears with Dan and ask for help, until she became aware of how her fears and insecurities dominated her. Mary's low dream was active and shaping her experience long before she acknowledged it. Once acknowledged, she was able to stop feeding it and take steps in a different direction.

Exercise 1.4

High and Low Dreams

Use the following exercise to reflect on your high and low dreams. Record your reflections in your journal.

1. Recall a relationship with an individual.

   - What is your high dream (your highest hope) for that relationship? What would it feel like to be with them? What would you be accomplishing together?
   - What is your low dream (your nightmare) for that relationship? What's your fear about what it could feel like? What do you dread the outcome will be?
   - Repeat this exercise, reflecting on different relationships each time. Notice what stays the same or changes from relationship to relationship.

2. Recall a group, committee, or team you are a part of.

- What is your high dream (your highest hope) for your life and work together?
- What is your low dream (your nightmare) for your life and work together?
- If you are working through this book with a small group, reflect on your high and low dreams for that group. Record them in your journal and share them with each other at your next group meeting.

3. Think about yourself.

- What is your high dream for your life? What helps you dream that dream for yourself?
- What is your low dream for your life? What calls forth those fears in you?

Self-awareness can be developed. This skill comes more naturally for some than for others, but with practice it can be developed and honed by nearly everyone. For the sake of what we want for ourselves and for the relationships we are part of, the work is worth the effort. Once we are aware of where we are, what we're feeling, and what's important to us, we can make choices that move us towards our highest hopes.

Note

1. Helpful exercises, rituals, questions, and prayers for beginning and ending meetings can be found in the following resources: Rochelle Melander and Harold Eppley, *Growing Together: Spiritual Exercises for Church Committees* (Minneapolis: Augsburg Fortress, 1998), and Charles M. Olsen, *Transforming Church Boards* (Bethesda, Md.: Alban Institute, 1995). Both are helpful resources.

Chapter

Two | Practicing
Self-Management

"*T*his is just how I am. Maybe it's hereditary
or the result of life experiences, but what
you see and what I do is what you get. Don't expect me to be
different."

We applaud the honesty of the person who declares, "This
is who I am." Stands do need to be taken, boundaries honored, feelings clearly expressed. For declaratory comments
to be truly useful, however, they need to be shared with awareness and intention rather than from a place of reactive impulse. Impulsive, unconscious, just "letting it all hang out"
expressions of emotion do not serve self or others. They separate people and put them on the defensive. Clear and straight-
forward words and actions made by choice and guided by an
awareness of purpose foster connection and right relationships.

Choice: A Fundamental Affirmation

Even when life presents us with circumstances beyond our
control, we can choose how we respond. Throwing up our
hands and declaring ourselves helpless is itself a choice.

We don't believe that people are helpless to control their
emotions and impulses. Though genes and life experiences
powerfully influence us, we affirm a person's free will and

ability to make choices. People possess the power to make choices about how they will respond. Self-management makes it possible.

We can manage our perspectives, emotions, and actions in the face of both internal forces and external circumstances. Our choices either honor or dishonor our values and high dreams. With the power of choice comes the responsibility for our experience of life. In addition, we have responsibility for helping shape the relationships we are part of. We cannot control our circumstances, but God has given us choice so that we can live authentically and creatively in the midst of those circumstances.

Definition and Importance of Self-Management

"Know thyself . . . and to thine own self be true." People often recite those two separate phrases from Socrates and Shakespeare's *Hamlet* as a single quote. They seem to belong together. The combination expresses the linkage between self-awareness and self-management. Self-awareness allows us to know who we are: our gifts, our limitations, our hopes, dreams, and fears.

Knowing those things, however, makes little difference if we cannot act in ways that honor them. Self-management is the developed "muscle" that allows us to stay true to our deepest values and highest aims, rather than be swayed by passing whims or fleeting fears. Our definition of the word *self-management* is making choices regarding our perspectives, feelings, and actions that support our values, our dreams, and our understanding of God's dream for us and for the world.

Self-management—making choices regarding our perspectives, feelings, and actions that support our values, our dreams, and our understanding of God's dream for the world

This chapter addresses three basic components of self-management: commitment, perspectives, and feelings. Commitment to our dreams provides the motivation for managing our perspectives and feelings. What do we want to achieve?

What results do we want? How committed are we to stepping into that vision? A high commitment to our dreams for us and our world provides both the criteria and the motivation for making wise choices about what perspective to hold and how to express our feelings.

Management of our perspectives and feelings does not mean denying, ignoring, or marginalizing them. Management instead means recognizing and acknowledging perspectives and feelings so that choices can be made about what emotion to express and how to express it. The goal is to be able to act in accordance with the impact we want to have on others and the work. Self-management puts us in a position to choose how to use the thoughts and feelings that are constantly swirling within us rather than to be used by them.

Self-management puts us in a position to choose how to use the thoughts and feeling constantly swirling within us rather than to be used by them.

Our perspective is the mindset we hold as we think about something. Perspective makes a difference. "I just want to get through this" has a different impact on us and the event than "I can't wait for it to begin!" Our perspective shapes our thoughts, attitudes, and even our feelings. It frames how we view a person or a situation and greatly determines our experience.

Feelings are our emotional response to our experiences in the world. Feelings are meant to be felt. Both pleasant and unpleasant, feelings provide us with information about how the situations we're in impact us. But if we cannot manage our emotions, they manage us. When we allow our emotions to control us, we are not at choice. Managing our feelings also means managing the intensity with which we feel and express them. Feelings felt and expressed with appropriate intensity are invaluable tools. When driving on a rainy night, a little bit of anxiety is a reminder to slow down and put more space between cars. Too much anxiety can have us freeze like a deer in oncoming headlights and severely compromise our driving skills at the very moment we need them most.

Managing our perspectives, feelings, and actions takes work, work that we may not feel eager about or up to doing. What pushes us to take a deep breath, rather than spit out an angry word, is the commitment to something bigger, something that we want more than the immediate gratification of unleashing our emotions. What lures us to step from the safety of the sidelines and express honestly what we think and feel is the commitment to something bigger than our fear of rejection.

Faith communities believe that God has dreams for our world and that God, through us, attempts to bring those dreams into embodied reality. Our commitment to God's work in the world provides the motivation to understand what God is trying to do through us. We are one of the vehicles through which God works. Self-management allows us to be clearer channels of God's creative Spirit.

The Power of Commitment to Our Dreams

Grounding ourselves in our dreams and God's dream is basic. A compelling vision of those dreams enlarges our view of what is possible and holds out a prize worth working for. Faith communities seek to teach people how to participate and partner with God in God's work. Faith communities provide a venue where people can submit their own values and dreamings to refining and shaping by the religious scriptures and teachings to which they adhere. These values and dreams are appropriately tested against historical, biblical wisdom found within the faith community. With that testing, we can more easily trust our dreamings as manifestations of God's intent for the world.

While the mere presence of vision makes a difference, it's the intent to live it out that makes a vision powerful. Commitment brings focus, presenting us with a clear aim to work toward and provides clarity about when to say yes and no. It was mid-afternoon on Wednesday. In light of a busy week, Craig had made a firm commitment to finishing his sermon before 9 P.M. that day—and the writing was coming slowly. That commitment helped him prioritize the various options for his afternoon and evening. In light of the deadline he had set for himself, it was clear that there were some things that he would have to say no to: no to attending Kiwanis, no to stopping by the youth-group meeting. At 8:30 that evening, with the sermon completed, Craig sank into his favorite chair with a sense of satisfaction. The week would be doable after all.

Commitment brings energy. As the small parts of life are aligned towards the keeping of deep commitments, synergy is created and progress occurs. A sense of fulfillment comes as those things held most important and dear are honored.

The Judeo-Christian tradition says that God is active in our world, continually creating and recreating. Humans can either participate with that creative effort or hinder it. We have the opportunity to open the way for Providence to move. Many say, and we agree, that making a commitment towards our dreams invites God into the process in a new and fuller way. Our commitment invites the Divine to mold us in whatever way is needed. Sir Edmund Hillary, climber of Mt. Everest and explorer of Antarctica, wrote:

> *Making a commitment towards our dreams invites God into the process in a new and fuller way.*

> Until one is committed there is hesitancy, the chance to draw back, always ineffectiveness. Concerning all acts of initiative (and creation) there is one elementary truth, the ignorance of which kills countless ideas and splendid plans; that the moment one definitely commits oneself, then Providence moves too.[1]

What are your deepest longings and your dreams for your faith community? What is your vision? What truly is important to you as you connect most deeply with what you value? The following exercise invites you to do some dreaming and assess your level of commitment to those dreams.

Exercise 2.1

Guided Meditation

Have your journal handy for making notes. If you are reading this out loud to a group, read slowly, pausing often. If you are trying this exercise on your own, you first might want to tape or read the guided meditation before doing it by memory.

Settle into a comfortable position, close your eyes, and take some deep breaths. Feel your weight being supported by the chair or floor and settle in, knowing that you are held and supported.

Become aware of a ball of white light within you. Notice as it begins to expand, spreading to more and more of your body, until it fills you, and you are filled with a sense of peace and comfort. The light begins to carry you to a new place. As you travel there, time slips away and you move into the future: 5 years, 10 years, 15 years. You now stand, 20 years in the future, outside the building that houses your faith community.

Still outside, notice the building and the setting. What do you see?

Now move inside. What are you aware of? Who is there? What is happening?

Wander through this space and feel the energy of God's presence. As you come across groups of people, notice how they interact with one another.

You notice a figure walking towards you. It is your future self—the person who, with many others and empowered by God, provided the leadership that allowed this faith community to find its way into this future.

Your future self greets you warmly. Notice what your future self looks like, what your future self is wearing, notice the expression on your future self's face. Your future self knows intimately your life and the journey that you are on—knows the struggles, knows the joys, knows what is possible. Your future self is a person of deep wisdom.

Ask your future self the following questions:

- What has God done here?
- What did it take for the people to reach this place?
- What was required of you?
- What did you have to commit yourself to?
- What has been most fulfilling for you personally?
- What do I need to know as I go back to walk this path?
- If there is another question you have of your future self, ask it now.
- Your future self looks at you with eyes of love and offers you a piece of wisdom to guide you. What is that piece of wisdom?

It's time to leave, but know that you can return here anytime you need to. Thank your future self for the wisdom and presence, and say good-bye.

Feel the ball of white light growing within you again. Allow it to carry you from that place back through time and into this present moment. Feel yourself returning to your body and this room. Become aware of your breathing and the sounds around you, and open your eyes.

Take a moment to jot down in your journal any notes you need to make. Use the following questions to reflect on the experience:

- What were the key elements of the vision of your future faith community? How is that an embodiment of God's dream?
- What was your role in the faith community becoming what you saw?
- What did you have to commit yourself to?
- On a scale of 1 to 10, how committed are you now to that vision?
- What would it take to move your commitment level up a notch? Three notches? If it's already a 10, what would shift it to a 15?

Our personal dreams give us a picture of our deepest values lived out. When we allow our dreams to interact with the dreams of others and the dreams of God, something new is created. That new creation is the life and soul of the faith community. A creation always reflects something of its creator. Looking at the life and soul of the faith community gives us insight about God, but also about ourselves. The state of our faith community mirrors our values and the commitments we have made or not made, giving us the opportunity to make adjustments or changes in what we bring to that place. Such shifts enable the faith community to embody more fully the life, health, and creativity of God. When the faith community is life-giving, it gives life back to us and passes it on to others. The health and generativity of our faith communities stem from our willingness and ability to commit to our dreams.

Managing Our Perspectives

Conventional wisdom posits that perspective is everything; we tend to agree. Our perspective is the window through which we choose to view another person, a situation, or the world in general. It determines what we see and how we see it. It is natural for individuals to form particular points of view about events, other people, and life situations. The viewpoint or mindset we hold affects how we process information and experience reality. For example, Mary's mother believed that Chryslers were the best cars on the road. That perspective allowed her to appreciate the many fine attributes of Chrysler automobiles and heightened her sensitivity to the faults of other makes. At the same time, it blinded her to what was superior about other autos and lacking in Chryslers. Her perspective was like a pair of glasses that determined what she saw.

Our perspective determines what we see and how we see it.

We do it all the time in all kinds of situations. We have perspectives on events; Easter week is overwhelming. We have perspectives on people; Frances is out to get me. We have perspectives on life situations; raising adolescents gives you grey hair. Perspectives almost always contain some truth. And when we are entrenched in one, like Mary's mother with Chryslers, that is the only truth we can see or experience. Perspectives are not givens; we can choose what kind of mindset we will have.

How we think about people, events, and life situations makes a difference in how we experience them and interact with them. Whenever a person throws up his hands and says, "that's just the way it is," it's a strong clue that the person is trapped in a perspective. "It's going to be a battle," Eric declared, talking about an upcoming congregational meeting. He shook his head, "If they're looking for a fight, I'll give them a fight, but I'm really dreading this." Eric's meeting was four days away, but already he had a clear metaphor in his mind for how it would likely go. The battle metaphor pervaded his thinking: people were in camps, he needed to armor himself, it might be a fight to the death. Every time he thought about the meeting, his stomach hurt. He wished it could be different, but this was simply how things were.

> How we think about people, events, and life situations makes a difference in how we experience them and interact with them.

That's the power of a perspective when we're trapped in it. Once we set our mind in a particular direction, alternative ways of viewing the situation disappear and we are left with what feels like the one and only truth. Walls box in our mental capacity; we lose flexibility to consider options. And while there is always some truth to the perspective we're trapped in, there are always other ways of looking at the same situation that also have some truth to them.

Every perspective comes with costs and benefits. The benefits Eric received from his battle perspective were focused energy and feeling like a valiant warrior. The cost was the emotional toll and viewing congregants as mortal enemies. Eric also had to give up his dream of the church as a place of reconciliation and healing. He didn't like looking at things that way, but in his mind that was the truth of the situation.

Eric noticed that he was holding a particular perspective on the meeting and decided he would look at some alternative mindsets that might serve him better. Noticing the sports page on the table and remembering how competitive his church was, he first chose to think about the meeting from the "Super Bowl" perspective. As he imagined the meeting from that mindset, he found himself smiling a bit and feeling energized. He appreciated the more positive energy, but as he thought about the costs of that perspective, he knew that it still promoted winners and losers, and that people get hurt even when it's a game.

Stepping out of that perspective, Eric saw his cat sleeping on the chair, one eye open and watching him. He wondered what the "sleeping cat" perspective might be. The cat was both relaxed and keeping a close eye on everything going on. He looked at the meeting from that viewpoint and noticed that he was breathing more slowly and felt calmer. Things might go just fine, but he would keep one eye watching for trouble just in case. He noted that in this perspective in addition to the calmness, he felt more distance from the other people and also a certain wariness.

Next Eric saw his daughter's building blocks on the floor. Let's try the "building block" perspective, he thought—children learn by building things, tearing them down and using the old parts to build new things. What if the tension we are feeling is just part of the process of building and rebuilding things—part of how we will learn? In this perspective, Eric felt curious about what would happen at the meeting and a little eager. To really hold this mindset, he would have to let go of needing to know how things would turn out. He would also need to let go of the need to be right.

Eric could have tried on many more perspectives, finding out what each felt like, what each provided, and what each required. Eric decided that the "building block" perspective would serve him better than the mindset of heading to battle. He picked up one of his daughter's blocks and kept it on his desk the rest of the week as a reminder.

Exercise 2.2

Choosing a Perspective

Reread the above story of Eric, noticing how he becomes aware of his initial mindset and how he surfaced other ways of looking at the situation and tried them on. Now, try it yourself. Have your journal available so that you can record thoughts and observations.

1. Think about an event or task that you are not looking forward to.

   - What is it about the event or task that you are not looking forward to?
   - How do you view it?
   - Sum up your viewpoint in a word or short phrase. Note that perspective in your journal.

2. Now think of five other perspectives you might hold on the same event or task. Imagine trying on different pairs of glasses, each one allowing you to see the event or task in a totally new way. Know that you are only trying on each set of glasses, not making a commitment to a perspective at this point. Here are some perspectives you might try on:

   - What would be the mindset of one of your heroes? A child you know? A trusted friend? A family member?
   - Be creative, even playful—look around the room and see what your eye falls on: a shelf of books, an open window, your shoes. What would the "bookshelf" perspective be on the task or event?

   As you imagine the task or event from each perspective, reflect on the following questions and again record your thoughts.

   - Notice what happens to your body as you try on this perspective. Does it tense? Relax?
   - What are the benefits of looking at the task from this perspective?

- What would you have to let go of to look at it this way?

3. After trying on five new perspectives, decide whether the one you started with still serves you best, or whether you want to commit to holding a new one.

4. Stand up and imagine a line in front of your toes. On the other side of that line is that new perspective, the one that will serve you best. When you are ready, step across the line as a way of committing to this new perspective.

Commitment to our vision and God's vision is foundational. To move towards embodying that vision requires making choices about our perspectives. It also requires making choices about what we do with our feelings.

Managing Our Feelings

Just as the perspectives we hold lead us to feel certain ways about people and circumstances, our feelings influence our perspectives. Anxiety over an upcoming meeting tinted everything pastor Hal looked at. The more he fretted about the meeting, the more uneasy he became about all that he faced at work and home. As his anxiety grew, others picked up on it. The mood in the office grew tense and the dinner table became strained. Our feelings impact us and the people around us. Whether or not we are aware of our emotional state, it gets communicated to other individuals and the groups we are part of, and has more power than our words.

Those who study communication say that our words convey only 10 percent of the message we send others. Tone of voice and body language carry the bulk of the content. Writing out our statements does not guarantee that is the message others will hear. Well thought-out statements only convey their intended message to the extent that our tone of voice and our mannerisms match our words.

Jerry trembled as he stood in the pulpit on Sunday morning. In two weeks, the congregation was hosting a controversial regional event. The event raised strong and differing opinions within the congregation. Though it demanded no decisions or actions on their part, simply the awareness that it would be held in their building caused tension among the members. Anxiety ran high that Sunday morning. Jerry offered all the right scriptural passages and theological concepts to frame the issue. He chose words designed to provide calm reassurance. And if those words had been printed and distributed, they might have had the intended effect. But Jerry's posture, facial expressions, tone of voice, and pace of speech sent a conflicting message. What he communicated under his words was deep anxiety and fear. People heard that and the conversations during coffee hour following the service were even more worried and fretful.

Feelings are contagious, especially the feelings of those in leadership roles. This makes the managing of them even more important. Becoming aware of and acknowledging the feeling is the first step. Once aware of our emotions, we can decide what to do with them. In the above story, Jerry could have done several different things. He might have chosen to acknowledge his own anxiety and used himself as an example of what a faithful response to anxiety is. Or, he might have spent time before the service addressing his anxiety so that it no longer controlled him.

> *Feelings are contagious— especially the feelings of those in leadership roles.*

We may not be able to eliminate certain feelings, but to a great extent we can control the intensity with which we feel them. Think of a light on a rheostat that can be dimmed or brightened. Similarly, we can amplify or tone-down our feelings, and thus amplify or tone-down the effect they have on us and others. Once we are aware of a feeling, simply focusing on it will intensify the feeling. Focusing on our irritation can expand a minor annoyance into

> *The first step in managing feelings is acknowledging them. Once aware of our emotions, we can decide what to do with them.*

a major frustration. Naming the emotion we are feeling and then turning our attention elsewhere often diminishes the intensity.

Mary doesn't mind flying as long as the ride is smooth. Storms and turbulence frighten her. Before when turbulence would hit, she would put her book down, take some deep breaths, and look around at the flight attendants and other passengers to see their reactions. Focusing her attention on the turbulence and her anxiety increased her uneasiness and fear. Because there is nothing she can do to change a rough ride, she decided to learn to manage her fear. Now when her plane hits rough air, she intentionally focuses her attention elsewhere, distracting herself with a book or movie. She has found that she can actually ignore a bumpy ride.

Sometimes feelings can hit with such intensity that they sweep us away. When an airplane is hijacked, the passengers and pilot are taken against their will to a place they did not choose to go. Our emotions can do the same to us. We blow up at a coworker, friend, or family member. Or, strong feelings seize us and we shut down, disengaging with the people around us. John had heard one too many wisecracks about his lateness in distributing minutes. A friendly jibe from Carolyn sent him over the edge. For the rest of the meeting John was so angry he disappeared into his own head, nurturing his resentful thoughts.

The impact of emotional hijacking on us and on others is significant. The discussion at the Wednesday leadership team meeting had been friendly and upbeat and the group was making real progress on designing a new initiative. A colleague asked Carla a reasonable question, seeking more information around what she was proposing. In a heartbeat, reality seemed to shift for Carla. Her body tightened

We can become hijacked by our emotions.

and, before she could stop herself, she let loose with defensive and sharp words. Carla responded as if she were the target of an inquisition, rather than part of a dialogue searching for clarity. Her teammates were surprised and Carla was too. Carla overreacted. And the odd thing was, she knew it as she was doing it, but couldn't seem to stop herself. She was emotionally hijacked by her own emotions.

Going back to Carla's story, her teammate may have been seeking simple clarification. Or, he may have indeed been seeking to discredit Carla's idea. It doesn't make a difference. In either case, Carla had a choice. She can speak and act in such a way as to create distrust and distance between her and her teammate and weaken the relationship, or she can speak and act in ways that invite understanding and connection and strengthen their relationship. It is possible to make a choice and stop an emotional hijacking.

The process begins with the self-awareness that a time-out is needed, claiming time to regroup, then intentionally choosing how we will hold ourselves and the other person. The following exercise is one way of releasing an emotional hijacking and connecting back to the person you want to be, an individual with a more excellent way—a way that is grounded in and creates a place of caring, honoring, and respect.

Exercise 2.3

Managing Emotional Hijacking

This first part will help you develop an awareness of those times when you get hijacked by your emotions. Keep your journal handy for note-taking.

1. Recall a time when strong emotions took you to a place you did not want to go and that was not useful.

   - What was the situation?
   - What was the emotion that hijacked you? (Such as anger, shame, jealousy, resentment, fear, etc.)
   - How did you respond?
   - What was the effect of that response?
   - What would have been a more useful response?

2. This next portion can take as little as 60 seconds. Practice it at least twice a day as you are emotionally hijacked in little ways; for example, a driver

who cuts you off in traffic, a rudeness at the grocery. Develop this muscle so it can be used as your default response at the first signs of being swept away by feelings.

The moment you feel yourself being swept away, call an internal time-out on your feelings. Imagine your hands actually forming the time-out signal. Imagine time slowing down and then stopping.

Take a deep breath and become aware of what is sweeping you away. Become aware too of the ground beneath your feet or the chair you are sitting in. Feel how solid it is and how it connects you to a sense of groundedness.

Shift your attention to your heart, becoming aware of the love, caring, acceptance, and honor found in your heart. Imagine those feelings moving further out through your body with each breath, each heartbeat. Allow the feelings of love, caring, acceptance, and honor to permeate your whole body. Repeat to yourself three times: "This is who I am at the core of my being."

Ask your heart the following question: "What is a more effective way to relate to this person or situation? What is the more excellent way?"

Respond to the person or the situation from the perspective of this more effective or excellent way.

The Impact of Self-Management

Our perspectives and feelings determine how we think about, interact with, and experience life. They not only impact us, they impact other people. When we walk into a room, our emotional state is experienced by others. Before any words are spoken, people pick up subtle clues about how we are and how to be with us. We ask ourselves, "Do I need to be cautious or guarded? Can I be open and teasing? Will my saying something trigger a response I don't want?" We have power that we are unaware of. How we "be" is just as important as what we do. People are pulled down or lifted up by our presence. Our perspectives and feelings can lead people to feel safer and more able to contribute, or ignored and marginalized.

Perspectives and feelings are contagious. We "pull" others toward being in sync with us as others also pull us. Clocks with swinging pendulums, when placed in the same room, move towards synchronization. This phenomenon, termed entrainment, seems to be prevalent throughout nature. Entrainment also occurs in groups, too. Our perspectives and emotions have influence even when we may think they do not, even when we tell others to pay no attention to us.

A person able to self-manage her feelings and perspectives can respond creatively to new information and unforeseen developments. Wilma had spent three months putting together a proposal for the judicatory board. A week before the presentation date, a sub-group of another team came to see her proposing a radically different approach. Wilma took several

> *Our perspectives and emotions have influence even when we may think they do not, even when we tell others to pay no attention to us.*

deep breaths. Reminding herself of her commitment to help her judicatory regain health, she overcame the impulse to throw them out of her office. Listening intently to what they had to say, she discovered their proposal provided an elegant solution to an aspect of the project she had been unable to solve. Together, she and they rewrote the proposal, resulting in a far superior product. Wilma's ability to self-manage made this possible.

Our ability to self-manage affects the work of the groups with whom we work. When we do not self-manage, others are placed in a position of having to manage us, taking time and energy away from the tasks at hand. Creativity diminishes. Enthusiasm fades. Rather than building safe and courageous space that welcomes what God's

> *When we don't self-manage, others are placed in a position of having to manage us, taking time and energy away from the tasks at hand.*

Spirit brings into the group, the team attends simply to maintaining civility, cautiously measuring words. Openness and adventure suffers, and God's dreaming fails to find full expression and embodiment in the group.

Alison walked into the weekly staff meeting and the conversation immediately shifted. Something on her face let everybody know that Alison was in one of her moods. This would be another one of those days of managing Alison. They would hold nonurgent questions for another time and certainly not bring up new projects for her approval. Work slowed down on days like this, but at least everyone got out alive.

When group members can each appropriately manage their perspectives and feelings, energy shifts and the team has the chance to move to places and accomplish things only dreamt of. People who are in conscious and intentional relationship with themselves are far more able to create conscious and intentional relationships with others.

Note

1. W. H. Murray, *The Scottish Himalaya Expedition* (London: J. M. Dent & Sons, LTD, 1951).

Chapter Three | # Social Awareness

Getting to Know Someone Else

The previous chapters focused on developing greater self-awareness and increasing our ability to manage our actions and reactions. Self-awareness and self-management are important accomplishments, allowing a person to function more effectively in society; however, they are only the initial steps as we prepare to be with other people. It is time now to look up and begin seeing our neighbor: that person sitting next to us—the person God has given to us for right relationship.

Chapter 4, "Learning to Love," focuses on our interaction with others and developing the ability to see them as gifted and beloved children of God. Before we can really appreciate and interact authentically with the persons sitting across from us, however, we have to see who they truly are. Without the intentional work of getting to know an individual, that person remains the creation of our own imagination. Our relationship is then with a projection we have created and not a flesh-and-blood person.

In this chapter, we look at the important and often overlooked step of learning about our neighbors. Unless we learn who they are and what they care about, we cannot really love them. The wisdom of this seems so evident and simple that it should go without saying, and yet experience says this step rarely occurs. When we do not take the time to get to know someone, right relationship simply does not happen. People perhaps experience polite interaction but authentic and holy connection eludes them. This chapter breaks down, into baby steps, how we get to know someone: setting aside our assumptions about him or her, becoming curious, and then listening and learning.

Ways to get to know someone:
- *Set aside assumptions*
- *Become curious*
- *Listen and learn*

Letting Go of Assumptions

Right relationship depends on knowing to the best of our ability not only who we are but who the other person is. What makes it difficult is that we often think we already know that other person, his likes and dislikes, his aims and goals, even, at times, what he is thinking and feeling.

As children we were naturally curious, linking observations with the question, "Why?" "Why do you have to go to work?" "Why does rain fall down?" "Why does John make that face when Mrs. Adams calls?" As we get older we tend to lose our curiosity. Now, rather than asking *why* someone makes a face when Mrs. Adams calls, we typically form a hypothesis in our minds and take that hypothesis as truth, without checking to see if we are correct. In other words, we make up stories.

Recounting the event to someone, we might say, "Mrs. Adams called John today. I didn't hear the conversation, but from John's face, I know he's really fed up with her. I'm certainly not going to suggest she serve on that task force." Three steps occurred. We saw an expression on John's face, we attributed a particular meaning to that expression, and then we responded and created an action plan based on that understanding. Problems do not arise, as long as the meaning we attached to the face John made is a correct interpretation. Without being curious and checking with John about the meaning of the face he made, however, we are acting on a made-up story.

Before we can really get to know other people, we have to let go of the stories we have made up about them. Within a few moments of meeting someone, we often put people in a basic category. Almost instantly we decide whether they are like us or not like us. If we see them as being like us, then, as we turn to them it is natural to take all of those things we know to be true about ourselves and apply them to the person next to us. If we adore having a fuss made about our birthday, we will probably assume that the person sitting across from us does too. If we see that the other person is not like us, we will likely attribute things to the person that are different from what is true for us. For instance, if we value tradition, we might find ourselves assuming that the other person, who seems so different, cares little about it.

The fallacy lies in thinking that by knowing ourselves and remembering what we have known about others, we know this new person. The person only needs to say a few sentences and we begin to categorize him. Pastor Doris was a short round woman with a loud voice. Harry, on the staffing committee, only had to hear her voice in their brief initial meeting to know that she was just like his mother, opinionated and bossy. He and this new pastor would never get along. Categorizing is a natural human response, allowing us to instantly decide how to relate and respond

> *We categorize people within moments of meeting them.*

to a new person. The problem comes when we believe that the initial categorizing gives us an accurate and full picture of the person and we invest no more time or energy in looking further.

We do a similar thing when our minds jump ahead and we fill in the blanks as people speak. Knowing what we do of the person, and knowing how we feel about the issue at hand, we listen just long enough to think we know where the person is heading. While that person is still talking, but before we fully understand what she is trying to communicate, we begin forming our response. Or, we hear someone using words that sound similar to what's true for us and we assume it's the same for the other person, "I know exactly what you're talking about," we say in agreement. The truth is, we don't.

What we think we know about others leads us to make up stories about their feelings and intentions. We take a comment and make up a story based on very little—a simple word or an innocuous action. It is particularly problematic when those stories are created through the lenses of our low dreams, reflecting our fears and worst thoughts. Janet, an older woman, did it recently with Evan, a younger colleague whom she did not know well. They had scheduled a phone conversation for noon. Janet called precisely at 12 P.M. No Evan. Janet instantly made up a story—Evan was irresponsible and had forgotten about the appointment. Or, some more interesting opportunity had come along and he had chosen to do that instead and didn't have the courtesy to reschedule.

We make up stories about a person's feelings and intentions and hold them as truth.

Three minutes later, Evan called—another scheduled appointment had run late. But in the space of three minutes, actually in a flash of an eye, Janet made her assumptions and decided that they were true. Curiosity about what happened was replaced by a made-up story about Evan's feelings and intentions.

Assumptions, the stories we make up about each other, separate us. When the stories come from our fears and anxieties, we make others into villains, attributing to them thoughts and feelings which may be far from true. Assumptions coming from our desire to elevate a person can blind us just as powerfully. People sometimes expect clergy leaders to be godlike and perfect. Assuming perfection, when the truth of the clergyperson's human flaws emerges, people experience disillusionment. This happens anytime we put people on a pedestal. Assumptions build walls rather than bridges. They prevent us from seeing and getting to know the actual person next to us.

Exercise 3.1

Awareness of Assumptions

1. Think of a group of which you are a member.
   Recall each person one by one, holding an image

of the person's face in your mind. List in your
journal 10 things you know about each person.

2. Reflect on how you have come to know those
things.
   • Did the person share that information with you?
   • Did it come through another individual?
   • What have you observed firsthand that leads
     you to believe this about the person?

3. Look at the list of 10 things you know about each
person. Which ones might be assumptions on your
part?
   • What are other assumptions you may be making
     about the person's attitudes and feelings?
   • How do those assumptions impact the way you
     relate to that person?
   • Are there some assumptions you need to check
     out with that individual? How might you do that?

Developing Curiosity

We get to know people through curiosity. Curiosity leads us
first to learn some basic facts about their lives. Where were
they born? Which foods do they like? Are they hot weather
or cold weather people? Curiosity, then, leads us beyond the
basic facts to wonder: What's really going on inside of them?
What is life like as seen through their eyes? What are their
dreams? What really is important to them?

Curiosity often plays a minimal role in discussions. One
person lays her thoughts on a subject on the table and then
backs up, allowing someone else to lay his thoughts out.
People politely listen and then offer their ideas. Positions are
taken and the ideas on the table debated. There is a decided
lack of curiosity about the deeper interests that give rise to
the positions people hold and defend.

At the end of a typical discussion, we may know the position a person holds on an issue, but we are no closer to knowing the person. What is behind or underneath that position

they defend so fervently? What values are being lifted up as important? What dream does this position serve? Getting to know someone means learning what that person thinks about things; it also means learning why that person thinks it.

In some settings, expressing curiosity about a person's deeper interests is considered side-tracking or rude. In a meeting, the mindset may be to "get the necessary business done as quickly as possible." Questions that probe deeper often meet with resistance and are viewed as irrelevant or a waste of time. Sometimes questions are not asked out of a desire to be polite. We tell ourselves that if there's something that person wants or needs to share, she will; it's rude to probe further.

In getting to know someone, we learn what that persons thinks and feels and where those thoughts and feelings rise from.

As coaches and consultants, we see the results of squelching curiosity in meetings. Participants leave, marginally committed to the decisions made and feeling a lack of connection to the other members of the group. What a tragedy! We miss the opportunity to connect heart to heart in the midst of work and create an experience of the kindom of God. The simple practice of curiosity could make a world of difference.

The Importance of Curiosity

When we talk, our words are a personal shorthand that sums up what we are thinking and feeling. Our verbal shorthand allows us to concisely convey thoughts and experiences and permits easy and flowing conversation. At the same time, it allows us to skip along the surface of a person and come away thinking we know that person well, when we do not. Emily was chatting with an acquaintance on the phone yesterday. The person commented, "It's such a lovely day." Those five words let Emily know her friend was experiencing the day as lovely, but not what made it lovely. Simply asking, "What makes it lovely for you?" would have given Emily deeper insight into her friend. Was it the sunny and warm weather that pleased her? The fact that the conflict in the congregation was diminishing? Perhaps it was the imminent arrival of her grandchildren. Or had she just received good test results from the doctor? Unless Emily asks, she can only imagine.

The first step in being curious is looking over at the other person, finding something that intrigues you or that you realize you don't know, and asking about it. The following exercise may seem a bit silly. We invite you to take it lightly and playfully. It is a way for a group to begin practicing curiosity with each other.

Curiosity–*asking about what intrigues you*

Exercise 3.2

Practicing Curiosity

At the beginning of your group meeting, agree that each person will practice curiosity three times during the meeting, turning to a person in response to a comment and asking a question in order to better understand the meaning behind the person's comment. Agree also that at least two follow-up "curiosity" questions will be asked in each case, probing more deeply for the meaning intended by the person. If you cannot think of follow-up questions, ask other group members to help you.

Good curious questions cannot be answered yes or no. They do not judge, but seek understanding and clarity. Here are some examples for starters:

- "John, your eyes lit up when you said that. What is it that's got them doing that?"
- "Sarah, you said this project feels exciting. What makes it exciting for you?"
- "LaTisha, you've used the word *commitment* four times tonight. What does that word mean to you?"

At the end of the meeting, take time for each person to respond to the following questions:

- How did asking curious questions impact you, the group, and your work?

- How did it feel when people asked you curious questions? Comfortable or uncomfortable?
- How could the other person have asked curious questions in a more helpful way?
- What was it like asking curious questions?
- What made it easy? Difficult?

Taking the Risk

Using our curiosity to get to know someone is so important. It leads us to invite the other person to share some of who

Curiosity communicates that we are interested.

they are with us. At the same time it tells that person that we see them and are interested in them. And yet, we seldom ask those curious questions. The reasons vary from person to person.

Sidney was part of a short-term spiritual growth group. Recently retired, he was looking for ways to connect with people with whom he could relate on a deeper and more intimate level. Every Wednesday afternoon, the group reflected on a piece of scripture, sharing their interpretations of the verse and what it meant to them. They quietly and politely listened to each other, speaking when it was their turn. Sidney ended the series feeling disappointed. He would lay out an opinion, longing for someone to be curious about why that was so and how he came to believe it. He longed for people to care enough about him to want to get to know him better. But it didn't happen. After each comment, people just smiled and nodded.

At first, he was disappointed in the group and the leader. Then, Sidney realized that he had not been any different than anyone else in the group. He had not extended himself to get to know any of them. He had not wanted to make himself vulnerable and extend an invitation to a deeper level of intimacy that might not be accepted.

It happened to Sarah just last week. While carpooling home from a gathering, she had the opportunity to chat with someone whom she had always found intriguing, but had never had a chance to get to know. They chatted for half an hour when Sarah realized that she was so busy thinking about how cool this was and wanting to be thought well of, that she was not really listening to what the person was saying. She had wanted so much to get to know this other person, but actually spent most of the time focusing on herself and her experience.

We hold back from really getting to know people for different reasons. Ralph had been a member of his small group for six weeks, but no one knew what he did during the day or the issues he faced there. Joe didn't ask because he thought that maybe Ralph was unemployed and that bringing it up would be a sore subject. Jennifer came from a culture that suggested it was impolite to ask about employment issues. Ginnie didn't ask because they were there to probe each other's souls and such mundane issues were of little importance. Randy, self-absorbed, never thought to ask. Each person in the group let something get in the way of his or her curiosity. Each of them, including Ralph, missed a simple opportunity to get to know each other better and missed the sense of connection that comes with that.

Listening to Words

Words provide a basic tool for relationships. They are how we communicate to others our experiences, our thoughts, and our feelings. Relationships can certainly be formed without words or language but there will be things never fully clarified or expressed. A recent newspaper article offers a painful example:

> Juliana Martinez Dionicio has no language. She is deaf and mute. Her family speaks only Trique, an obscure Indian language that is foreign even to other Mexicans. She communicates with her family in gestures no one else understands.
>
> Illiterate and silent, Juliana lives in isolation made even more profound by her circumstances—traveling

with her sister and father in an anonymous stream of undocumented immigrant farmworkers who tend fields across the West.

One cold day last November, the tiny 24-year-old climbed a rusty chain-link fence into a neighbor's filthy dog pen in Livingston, Calif. Alone, she gave birth to a baby girl.

Then she stuffed several wads of tissue in the infant's mouth.

California authorities arrested her on a charge of felony child endangerment.

"I would look at her sitting there in court and wonder what was going through her mind," said prosecutor Larry Morse II. "We can only suppose as to know she understands."

Imagine living in a world without words. Then imagine getting pregnant, perhaps as a result of rape, giving birth alone, being arrested—and not having the words to explain, or to understand what is happening.

That is Juliana's story.[1]

The ability to communicate through language is such a gift to right relationship. Forming right relationships and developing trusting community, however, requires more than just access to words. The way words are used and the intent behind them make a tremendous difference. Words can heal or hurt, fostering intimacy between people or destroying it. Words can be used to defend positions and score points, as in debate. They can function as weapons, to demean and humiliate. And, words can just be words, noise to fill the silence. Alone, words are neither good nor bad, but a tool. Right relationship demands the proper use of words as a tool.

Words can heal or hurt, fostering intimacy between people or destroying it.

Words open a window into a person's mind and heart, providing the opportunity to hear and understand another person's thoughts, experiences, and feelings. Our words and tone of voice invite sharing when they are respectful, honoring, and curious. The proper use of the tool of words requires both our attention to the words of others and attention to the words we use.

Listening at a certain level comes naturally. Deep listening, however, takes practice. Natural habits often work against us. A common habit is filling in the blanks. On Dan's Internet browser, when he starts to type in an address, the browser automatically fills in the rest, sometimes incorrectly. We do the same thing when we listen to others. We hear just enough of a person's words to allow us to conclude that we understand what is meant. Nodding our head and verbally responding, "Yes, I understand," elicits a satisfied response from the speaker. It cues the speaker that no more explanation is needed. Both the speaker and we assume there is a common understanding on that issue. What a great surprise it is later when we all discover the great distance apart we are on the very topic on which we assumed we agreed.

Preparing our response while the other person still speaks makes it impossible to really hear what the person says. We listen long enough to get the gist of the idea, and then we begin forming our reply. Nodding and making "I'm listening" noises to the speaker, we are actually lost

> *Hindrances to listening include the following:*
> - *Filling in the blanks*
> - *Preparing our response*
> - *Our own perspectives*

in listening to ourselves and have lost our connection to that person.

Our perspectives can also hinder our ability to listen. Our understandings of the meaning of words and experiences get in the way of hearing what they mean to someone else. We automatically filter everything another says through our own perspective. Only through great effort do we set aside our perspective and see things from the perspective of the other person. Good, focused listening opens the way for really seeing and getting to know what is important to another person.

"Getting this situation solved is critical," Jack declared. Really wanting to understand Jack, Andy let go of his understanding of why he thought solving it was so important and asked, "Critical? How?" Andy was glad he did. Not only was Jack's view of what made it critical vastly different than Andy's take, so was what Jack meant by "this situation." That one misunderstanding would have caused buckets of problems later on, had they not caught it. Careful listening on Andy's part helped each understand what was important to the other and avoid misunderstandings.

Good listening also leads to a greater understanding of the core interests that lay behind a person's words. When a person expresses an opinion, such as, "Worship should be at 10 A.M.," what is the deeper interest behind that comment? Does it reflect a deep valuing of tradition? Perhaps . . . and perhaps not. We don't know until we ask the question, "What's important to you about it being at 10 A.M.?" That person's answer tells us a lot about him or her, providing insight into those things that are most important to the person.

Community, connection, and right relationship happens through focused nonjudgmental listening. Deep listening is transformational, touching all involved in a profound way.

Good listening leads to a greater understanding of the core interests that lie behind a person's words.

Much can be learned about listening from Alcoholics Anonymous. The rule, "no cross talk," defines the way to participate. As a person talks, telling his or her story of struggles, failures, successes, and longings, the rest of the group can only listen—no comments either while the person is talking or after he or she is finished. There are to be no reactions or questions to the person. The group simply moves on to listen to the next person who chooses to speak.

The "no cross talk" rule quiets the chatter in listeners' minds. There is no working on what to say in response, no watching for an opportunity to cut in. Each word is a treasured clue to the unfolding of that person's life, the feelings, dreams that she or he is attempting to express, learn, and live into. As significant dreams, tragedies, and victories are expressed, the sharing takes on a sacred quality. The sense of sacredness stems as much from the deeply respectful and appreciative listening going on in the room, as from the honesty and depth of sharing of the speaker.

The "no cross talk" principle helps us listen without preparing our own response. However, having done that careful listening and with the objective of doing work together, we must take a step further and enter into dialogue. Having listened so carefully, and beginning to catch a glimpse of the sacred essence of the person, we to want to see and know more. Comments raise questions in our minds and we want clarification and expansion so we can more fully understand this person. Sensing the depth of the person, we long to ask questions so that more of their divine essence is revealed. That's not the purpose of AA. It is, however, part of the purpose of a faith community.

Asking curious questions requires letting go of our assumptions and our judgment. Listening deeply takes effort and practice. Both are worth it. Having been given the gifts of words and a common language with which to express them, we have the opportunity to use words to explore the heart, mind, and soul of another. Juliana did not have words. We do, and they are an important tool in right relationship.

Paying Attention to Signals

Only a fraction of what people are trying to convey is initially carried by their words. Tone of voice, facial expression, and body language transmit much of the message. As discussed in chapter 1, we refer to those nonverbal yet observable ways of communicating as signals. Just as we can listen to a person's words, we can listen to what they say nonverbally. "Listening" to signals provides clues about what a person may be thinking or feeling. People are often unaware of the signals they send. Gestures and facial expressions are

> Tone of voice, facial expression, and body language provide clues to what a person thinks and feels.

usually unconscious movements that signal how a person is feeling and what she or he is thinking. What is going on in someone's mind and heart is often first glimpsed through that person's nonverbal communication. Sometimes signals point to thoughts and feelings the speaker is not fully aware of yet.

A person's nonverbal expressions carry meaning, but only that person knows exactly what. We can guess, but until we ask, we really do not know. The clearest and easiest way to find out the meaning of a signal is to ask. Notice something, for example, a gesture that seems to stand out to you, and get curious about it. It might be, "What are those tapping fingers saying?" or "Tell me about those tears" or "You keep scrunching up your face. What's that about?"

A person's gestures, facial expressions, and voice tones can amplify what the speaker is verbalizing. Or, they can stand in contradiction to their words. People communicate far more nonverbally than they do with their words. Exploring signals can lead to deeper understandings of what people think and feel and can help take a conversation to a much deeper level.

For a week or so, whenever Erica talked about moving ahead on a particular project, she got very vehement and Jeff didn't understand her intensity. When they would talk about it, Erica would move her right forearm up and down in a slow chopping motion. Finally noticing it, Jeff asked her about it, "You keep making this motion [and he demonstrated it] whenever we talk about this project. What's this motion about? Are you trying to nail something down?" Erica kept doing the motion slowly and Jeff began doing it with her. After a few moments, her eyes went wide, "No, it's about this feeling I have that our pathway is getting pretty complex and we really have to stay focused on our goals. I am really committed to getting there and I'm a little concerned that you're going to get lured away with other projects. When I do this hand thing, I think I'm pointing to the vision and cutting through the distractions."

Noticing and inquiring about nonverbal signals help us understand better what a person is trying to communicate.

Jeff's asking about Erica's gesture surprised her. She was unaware she was doing it. Jeff seemed genuinely curious and when he began making the gesture himself, Erica got curious too. Something about seeing him do it made it easier for her to do the gesture. As together they repeated the motion over and over, Erica began thinking about the project and came to some important insights. She knew she had been feeling anxious, but had not been able to put her finger on why. "Funny," she thought. "My arm knew what was going on for me before my mind did!"

Sometimes the signals a person sends are incongruent with the words coming out of his mouth or even with another signal that person is sending. Using a clipped, cold tone of voice while saying "I'm sorry" is a double signal, signaling that in addition to feeling sorry, there are likely other things that person feels.

How do we know the meaning of someone's signals? We don't until we ask. Following up our observations with curiosity rather than assumptions lets the other person provide us with accurate interpretations of their nonverbal signals. "Sounds great, count me in." Those were Runi's words, but as she said them she turned away from the group and looked out the window. The group, hearing affirmation around the table, moved on with their business. Sheila, noticing that Runi seemed to be saying one thing with her words and another with her body, stopped them. In a gentle and curious voice she asked, "Runi, I noticed that when we made that last decision you turned away and started looking out the window. Are you okay?" Runi was silent for a moment. "I guess I'm feeling a bit run over, like it doesn't make much difference what I think." The others were surprised. Each had made up a different story for why she turned away from the group and looked out the window.

Bill thought she had heard a noise. Irma assumed she was checking out the playground which they would be talking about next. Sheila didn't really know, but she dared to ask. And her asking brought important information to the group and helped bring Runi back to the team.

The first step in learning to listen to signals is to notice them. As you move through your day, become aware of the gestures people use as they speak and the expressions they make with their faces. Having noticed them, get curious about them. That means, once again, letting go of assumptions and getting curious. Just because we know what is going on with us when we shrug our shoulders, does not mean we understand its meaning when another person does it. We have to drop our assumptions, get curious, and ask.

If the signal we are curious about is a gesture or a facial expression, it will help the other person if, as we ask, we demonstrate it. They may be totally unaware they are doing it. Seeing us do it allows them the opportunity to observe it and get curious themselves.

Exercise 3.3

Becoming Aware of Signals

The following exercise will help you notice and explore signals. Keep notes in your journal documenting what you discover. If you are reading this book with a group, share your experiences with the group at your next meeting.

1. When you are in the line at the grocery store, sitting on the bus, or some other place that gives you an opportunity to observe people, become aware of the people around you.
2. Without listening to people's words, notice their facial expressions, gestures, and tone of voice.
3. Notice the assumptions you make about what those signals mean.
4. Let go of your stories and get curious.
5. Imagine you know that person. In your mind, what signal are you most curious about? How would you ask about it?

Listening through Intuition

We are driving home when all of a sudden we think, "I really should give Eric a call." We have not thought about him in weeks and yet suddenly there he is in our thoughts. Later on, when we speak with him, we discover how well timed it is— there is indeed something going on in his life. Or, we are sitting next to someone in a meeting and we get this sense that the person is carrying around something heavy. We look over at the person and cannot see anything—it is just a feeling. After the meeting, we ask, "Everything okay?" and we find that nothing in that person's life right now is okay.

In addition to listening to words and to the nonverbal yet observable signals that people send, we listen to others through our intuition. Intuition is how we know things when we have not been told through words or signals. The Myers-Briggs indicator has helped us understand that intuition is as valid a way of gathering information as through our senses. Intuition is that out-of-the-blue hunch or funny nudge. It is knowledge, but a different kind of knowledge than that which comes from logic, reason, or our senses. All people have intuition to some degree and it is a muscle that can be strengthened.

Intuition is how we know things when we have not been told through words or signals.

Intuition is not as valued in our culture as linear reasoning and logic. Some dismiss intuition as unreliable. What may be unreliable is our interpretation of our intuitive nudges. For others, the word conjures up crystal balls and new-age psychics. Intuition is not mystical or magical, it is just another way of listening and gathering information about the person next to us.

Where do the intuitive "hits" come from and how do we explain them? How can we know that something significant may be going on in the life of the person next to us without words or physical, bodily signals? We don't know and leave it to others to discern and explain. We do know that when an "E" is played on the piano, the "E" string on the guitar sitting next to that piano will begin to vibrate. Intuition seems similar to that. Somehow at certain times we absorb and resonate with what someone else is experiencing. We listen to intuition not through paying careful attention to the words or signals of the other person, but by listening to ourselves and the vibrations or nudges within us.

Intuition invites us to connect with another person. "I'm not sure why, but you've been on my mind all week, so I thought I'd call." Intuition, in a case like that, is a nudge toward relationship. Something within us draws us forward to take a step that rationally, intellectually, may make no sense. The impact is often quite profound.

Just as signals can alert us to a person's inner thoughts, so can our intuition. It was an intuitive nudge that led Herb to look around the table and ask, "Is there something not being said here?" The discussion had been going smoothly and civilly and there was no sign that anything was wrong, and yet Herb just could not shake the feeling that there was something people were not saying. All it took was his question and the dam broke and weeks of frustration poured out.

Herb could have just as easily been wrong about his hunch. Voicing it still would have served the group, indicating that Herb was working hard to listen. It would have given them the opportunity to search themselves and find that there truly was nothing that they were holding back—a good thing both for the group and Herb to know.

> *Notice your hunch, voice it, and then let go of needing to be right about it.*

The important thing in that case would have been for Herb to notice his hunch, voice it, and then let go of needing to be right about his interpretation of it. Simply expressing our intuitive hunches indicates a desire and commitment to honor and hear all voices and build connection.

It is important not to be attached to the initial meaning we assign our hunches. Similar to the assumptions we make about words and gestures, we may well be wrong. We have to check it out. The point of listening intuitively is to hear what the other person is saying, rather than tell them what we think.

Something happens to the person experiencing the intuition of another person. They sense being seen and known in a different way. They report feeling cared about—that someone cared enough to take the time to notice and to ask. They often find that their connection with the other person seems stronger afterwards, as if a bond has been established that is deeper than the task at hand.

Norms and customs work against our nurturing and using intuition even though it can bring powerful benefits. Asking someone about something the person has not chosen to reveal could be viewed as impolite and disrespectful of a person's privacy and choices. It could be regarded as putting the person on the spot, making her feel uncomfortable. Another subtle but powerful reason persons may shy away from expressing intuition is that using intuition can also quickly take people to a more intimate level. It connects them at a feeling level. To know another person and to be known by another person at a level beyond words creates a powerful and deep connection. That kind of connection may not be comfortable.

How intuition is expressed is important. Gently expressing our sensing or wonderings without attachment to being right about them invites the other person to respond. The person may be aware of something and choose not to share it with us. So be it; that is her right. Or, the intuitive nudge that feels so strong in us may truly not resonate with her at all. Share intuitive nudges lightly and gently, and then let go of them.

> *Knowing another person and being known at a level deeper than words creates a powerful and deep connection.*

Intuition is simply a feeling on our part. That feeling carries with it no interpretation of the meaning or content. The interpretation is the meaning we give it. If our nudge is genuinely a connection with something in the other person, only that other person can provide the content, the interpretation. Always basic to the use of intuition is total respect for the other person. Anything less is a violation of something sacred.

The Impact of Knowing and Being Known

What is the impact of one person laying aside his assumptions, being genuinely curious about another person and listening? Dan recently experienced that very thing over a cup of coffee during a break in a meeting. Having recently retired, the question everyone had been asking was, "How's retirement?" He rarely had the chance to answer before people launched into how they could not wait for their retirement and all the things they planned to do. During this coffee break, Jim asked him the same thing.

Dan did not know Jim very well, and started to give him what had become his standard reply, "Oh, just great!" Something in Jim's tone of voice and the expression on his face stopped Dan. Jim appeared to be genuinely curious. Dan paused for a moment and then told what he had not dared tell the others—that it was a difficult transition. Without his defined work role, Dan doubted his usefulness to society and feared the emptiness he felt.

The way Jim listened made it easy to share. Dan felt truly seen for the first time since his retirement. He felt honored that someone genuinely wanted to connect with him as just a person and not a role. That 15-minute conversation affected Dan profoundly. First, he was no longer invisible and felt a new sense of hope that retirement would be just fine. Second, as the meeting continued on and Jim and Dan held differing opinions about the topic at hand, Dan found himself listening to Jim in a new way. He really wanted to understand where Jim's thoughts and feelings were coming from. It took very little from Jim—a simple question, asked in a caring and curious way followed by interested listening. Jim's desire to understand profoundly impacted Dan and the way they interacted for the rest of the day.

Getting to know the other person opens the way for love. Right relationship develops as we care enough to ask questions and listen. Lives shift and bonds form as we open ourselves to each other in new and deeper ways.

Note

1. Juliana Barbassa, Associated Press, "A World without Words and without Hope," *Los Angeles Times,* April 18, 2004.

Chapter
Four | **Learning to Love**

C ongratulations! You have noticed the persons God placed next to you and now know something about who they are and what they care about. Now comes what can feel like a very risky step—daring to love them. The Hebrew and Christian scriptures command us to move beyond "get to know our neighbor" and into "love our neighbor." Love demands we make choices about the values we uphold, the attitudes we adopt, and how we interact with others. Typically, we are not conscious of those choices.

Love: A Choice

Each relationship we are part of has its own unique quality. Some people we click with, some we grate against, and some we barely notice. Relationships often unfold haphazardly, without much thought or guidance. Whether we know it or not, however, we make choices that determine how we experience and interact with each other. Often our choices reinforce rather

> *Our choices determine how we experience and interact with each other.*

than alleviate the separation and distrust we experience with someone. This chapter addresses choices that help us better love all kinds of people, in all kinds of situations.

The loving way of relating brings life and fulfillment to each person involved. Julie's last conversation with her staff supervisor ended in a fight. As Julie prepares for a follow-up meeting with him, she knows she is defensive and ready to blame. Letting go of that attitude will not be easy for Julie. But for their relationship to recapture the mutuality and respect that Julie values, she knows she must find and choose a different way.

Popular culture talks about love in the romantic sense. The Judeo-Christian tradition, however, commands us to live out love in all of our relationships. "You shall love the Lord your God with all your heart, and with all your soul, and with all your might" (Deut. 6:5). "You shall love your neighbor as yourself" (Lev. 19:18). Our charge is to love. An old song by Will Young featured the recurring line, "Love the one you're with." Though the songwriter intended a different meaning, the line provides a fitting admonition for members of faith communities. "Love your neighbor" directs us to love whomever we are with, whether we like them or not.

The question from the Gospel of Luke in the Christian scriptures, "Who is my neighbor?" expresses a natural desire. Let me find someone I can naturally love and I will claim that person as my neighbor. The truth is that God gives us each person we encounter as a neighbor. Our neighbor is the person begging money outside the grocery store, the telemarketer who calls at dinner, and the person at the committee meeting who drives us crazy.

God gives us each person we encounter as a neighbor.

We struggle to find words to define how we love other people. Love is the subject of countless books and songs. It is clear that love is central to the faith we practice. We know love is more than a feeling, but when it comes down to exactly how to love someone, the water gets murky. Though commanded to love, the specific directions on how to do it are less than clear.

Six Essential Questions and Choices

We find six choices crucial for every relational interaction. These choices provide the groundwork for the relationship to be a loving relationship. These six choices make it possible for us to relate in loving ways and move toward fulfilling and life-giving relationships:

1. What do I want my relationship with this person to be like?
2. What attitudes and values do I want to honor as I'm with this person?
3. What must I let go of in order to turn towards this person?
4. What is the goodness in this person that I will see and trust?
5. How will I acknowledge to the person the holy goodness that I see in her or him?
6. What will I dare to ask of this person?

Discipline yourself to answer these questions as you prepare to be with people. These choices can enhance already good relationships and improve difficult ones. Practice making these choices with a variety of people. Over time, this process will become habit, done with unconscious competency. These six practices will strengthen all of your relationships and increasingly connect you in deep ways with others.

1. What Do I Want My Relationship with This Person to Be Like?

The pictures we hold in our minds about how interactions will go make a difference. In chapter 2 we discussed the power of high dreams and low dreams. High dreams reflect our greatest hopes and desires. Low dreams reflect our deepest fears and insecurities. Whichever one we choose to let fill our minds will shape the interactions we share with others. In order to engage in

Picture in your mind what right relationship would look like with the person.

right relationship, the first step is to picture in our own minds what right relationship would look like with that person.

In a troubled relationship or a relationship filled with tension, clarity about what we want becomes even more crucial. Commitment to our high dreams keeps us focused on what is most important to us. Carla thought her copastor John had responded in a dishonoring way to her input at the last board meeting. Carla was angry and hurt. She felt put down and started growing suspicious about his intentions. Was he trying to send her a message—maybe ease her out? Up until this point, she had enjoyed working with John and she wanted the partnership to continue in the same collegial and fruitful way.

She weighed in her mind different ways to approach John about his behavior at the meeting. The angry part of Carla wanted to storm into John's office and blast him. The hurt and embarrassed part of Carla wanted to tender her resignation and slink off. What she held in her mind was the picture of how creatively and enjoyably she and John had worked in the past. As Carla thought about it, she knew she wanted that for their future as well. To help remind her of her commitment to help make the relationship be that, she placed on her desk a picture of them laughing together. Carla knew she would have to confront John about his comment, but she was committed to doing it in a way that would foster good relationship.

While holding a picture of how we want things to be is important in strained relationships, it holds equal importance in relationships that are smooth and enjoyable. Every time we are with another person or a group of people it is a new experience. Fresh commitment to our dreams brings life and energy and keeps the relationship from slipping into being stale and boring.

When we are clear about how we want our relationship with another person to be, we know more clearly how to speak and act.

When we are clear with ourselves about how we want our relationship with another person to be, we know more clearly how to speak and act.

Exercise 4.1

How Do I Want This Relationship to Be?

Keep your journal handy to record thoughts and observations.

1. Recall a person with whom you have a relationship and will be with this week.
2. What are your highest hopes for how the interaction will go and what it will feel like?
3. What are your greatest fears for how the interaction will go and what it will feel like?
4. As you think about your upcoming meeting, are your expectations closer to your highest hopes or your greatest fears?
5. What is one thing you can do to keep your highest hopes more fully in front of you?

2. What Attitudes and Values Do I Want to Honor as I Am with This Person?

Once we know what we want our relationship with another person to be like, we must make a choice of how we will be with the person. Will I be a judging person? A blaming person? Will I stand in the place of skepticism? The place of cautious waiting? Or will I stand in the place of anticipation and openness? Will I be a learner? A nurturer? One who trusts? Each choice influences differently our words, our actions, and how we view the situation and the person we face. Each day we have the opportunity and responsibility to decide who we will be as we move through our activities and encounters.

The attitudes and feelings we bring with us help create what happens in our encounters. We have amazing power. When we walk into a meeting in a spirit of distrust, the group will begin to mirror that distrust. On the other hand, speaking from a perspective of understanding encourages others to do the same.

> *The attitudes and feelings we bring with us help create what happens in our encounters.*

We can choose from a multitude of stances in relating to people. Four in particular should be avoided, or stopped when they show up. These four stances are common responses, but research reveals they are devastatingly harmful if used regularly in a relationship. Termed by researcher John Gottman as the "Four Horsemen of the Apocalypse," they are criticism, contempt, defensiveness, and stonewalling. Interacting with others from any of these four places creates and magnifies distance and distrust.

In reviewing the annual financial campaign, Steve criticized Doris and Harry for the packets being mailed late. Harry immediately became defensive. Doris rolled her eyes and contemptuously commented that the materials Sally had produced were so poorly done that their late arrival made little difference. Sally sat in stony silence, refusing to interact at all. When we allow our reaction to a person to come from a place of criticism, defensiveness, stonewalling, or contempt, the unloving parts of ourselves are roused and called forth. Their appearance often triggers similar responses in those we are with. When we choose these stances, we suffer, others suffer, and the relationship between us suffers.

The four toxic stances are:
1. *Criticism*
2. *Contempt*
3. *Defensiveness*
4. *Stonewalling*

Other stances can bring life to a relationship, including understanding, playfulness, audacity, caring, compassion, and honoring. The choice of a love-based stance calls forth more positive stances from others. Four elderly women and their younger pastor stood in an empty sanctuary tensely staring at each other. On the walls around them were colorful life-size self-portraits of the congregation's children. They linked hands like paper dolls.

Stances that can strengthen a relationship include the following:
- *Compassion*
- *Playfulness*
- *Caring*
- *Audacity*
- *Respect*
- *Honesty*

Gertie, the chair of the altar guild, spoke firmly: "The drawings of the children have to come down. Tomorrow's Easter." The members of her committee nodded.

The pastor, stunned, blurted out, "But those children are part of us! They remind us of why we're here. Each new child added to the wall lets us all see the difference we're making and that our congregation is growing. They tell everyone who walks in that children are important here. They have to stay!" Gertie's eyes narrowed and she bit off her words: "Older members are important, too. What do you see in here that tells them that?"

The pastor took a deep breath, willing herself to calm down enough to hear the message underneath Gertie's words. She imagined putting on glasses fitted with lenses of understanding. Another breath and her vision shifted just enough to say, "You really care about the older members here." Gertie dropped her eyes and some of the fight seemed to go out of her. "I do. Easter is so important to them and they love how the sanctuary looks on that day." The conversation lasted another 30 minutes as the five women worked it out together. How we regard another person powerfully affects us, the other person, and the relationship.

Assuming a love-based stance does not mean putting on rose-colored glasses and blithely walking through the world. At times, hard truths must be spoken. Speaking the truth of our experience from a stance of love actually increases the chance that the other person will hear it. Right relationship demands that the hard and difficult things be shared, but in respectful and caring ways.

> *At times, hard truths must be spoken. A stance of love increases the other person's chance of hearing it.*

The following exercise gives you the chance to practice making choices about how you want to be with other people. It invites you to try out new perspectives in your mind as well as practice them. Document reflections from this exercise in your journal.

Exercise 4.2

How Will I Be with This Person?

1. Recall a person with whom you would like a strengthened, more loving relationship.

2. List 10 possible attitudes you could have as you regard that individual (such as curious, firm, honoring, playful, judging, honest, direct, caring, accepting, trusting, skeptical, collaborative, audacious, authentic, etc.).
3. Which ones of the 10 might create distance or distrust?
4. Which ones of the 10 feel more loving?
5. Of those that feel more loving, pick one that you will try. Throughout the next week, simply regard people from that perspective—all people, including the person you initially named.
6. As the week continues, note the impact on you, on others, and on the person.

3. What Must I Let Go Of?

In the first two choices, we named our hopes for the relationship and determined the attitudes and values we wanted to embody. Before we can really step into all of that, we must make an honest assessment of ourselves. What within us might hold us back from what we desire?

How might we, unwittingly, sabotage the results we want?

How might we, unwittingly, sabotage the results we want? As we commit to step further into right relationship, we need to become aware of the hidden attitudes, assumptions, and feelings that might get in our way.

Jane, the incoming president of the woman's group, looked forward to her new role. The previous president, Miriam, did all she could to help orient Jane. Jane appreciated Miriam's help and was grateful that she would be able to call on Miriam's expertise in the future. Jane envisioned their relationship as warm and mutually supportive. She tried to hold herself as competent and collaborative in her meetings with Miriam. She noticed, however, that she often held back her thoughts and ideas around Miriam, even to the point of avoiding talking about changes she would be making. Jane wondered why in the world she was doing this. Jane realized that a part of her was worried Miriam would feel marginalized and left out. "I'm acting like I don't trust her to be able to make this transition! How silly," she thought. "Miriam is one of the least fragile people I know." Jane came to understand that she had to let go of her worry about Miriam being able to move on.

That choice was not terribly difficult for Jane. Realizing how she was getting in the way of the relationship she wanted to create, she acknowledged her fear and set it aside. Sometimes the things we have to let go of are more deeply planted and require more from us. As hard as it might be for the sake of what we most deeply want, sometimes we must set aside past experiences and biases. Otherwise, our relationships remain unproductive and uncomfortable. We

> *For the sake of what we deeply want, sometimes we must move beyond past experiences and biases.*

may never forget the past, nor in some cases should we. The past can hold important lessons. The past must not hold us captive, however, preventing us from engaging in the present moment and creating a new future.

Cliff, new to the board of trustees, remembers well the occasion when Randy, also on the board, undercut him in the workplace setting they shared. The event happened several years ago, but it still ate at Cliff. Since they now worked in different divisions of the plant, Cliff had been able to avoid Randy at work. Polite when their paths did cross, a casual observer would not have known that Cliff held a grudge.

Now, here they were together on this small and important board of the congregation. Cliff watched Randy closely the first six months he served on the board. Nothing he saw and nothing he experienced from Randy was out of line. Nevertheless, Cliff's stomach churned every time he had to go to that meeting. Cliff decided he couldn't stand it much longer. He knew he would either have to resign from the board or let go of his resentment. He observed Randy closely for three more months and decided that he wanted to let go of that hurt. Randy truly seemed different now and Cliff valued serving on the board.

He wrestled then with whether he needed to confront Randy about the event four years prior or not. After several more weeks of weighing both options, he decided that the time had come and took a deep breath and let it go. Cliff's choice to let go of a past hurt was difficult for him. In the end, he decided that holding on to it kept him from the kind of life he wanted for himself. Across the next year Cliff got to know Randy. And while they didn't become close friends, Cliff developed an appreciation for Randy's gifts and even came to enjoy working with him on the board of trustees.

There are times when, unlike Cliff, we find we cannot set certain things aside without confronting in some way the person who hurt us. We are not advocating that you stuff real feelings. We are inviting you to release them. In instances like this, we must anchor ourselves in the outcome we want to work toward and the attitudes and values we want to embody. That anchoring will guide our difficult conversations. A compelling vision of the outcome we long for can give us the courage to speak up and share feelings that are difficult to speak. Sometimes the only way to move beyond past hurts is to face them, name them, and build agreements with the other person that shift hurtful ways of interacting. There are some experiences that may feel impossible to set aside and perhaps even some that should not be set aside. Some relationships fall into destructive enough patterns that the safest thing for all involved is to end the relationship. We hope those are the exceptions. In the majority of cases, the mandate to love requires us to find ways to acknowledge and move beyond the attitudes, feelings, and biases that separate us from others. This frees us to create new patterns for living in the present.

Exercise 4.3

Letting Go

Record thoughts and reflections in your journal.

1. Recall a person with whom you feel some distance or distrust.

- What contributes to that attitude or feeling in
  you?
- Imagine holding that attitude or feeling in your
  right hand.

2. Recall the loving perspective chosen in the exercise
   above (exercise 4.2). Imagine holding that perspective in your left hand.
3. With one perspective in each hand, consider them
   both. Bring to mind your deepest hopes for your
   relationship with this person.
4. Set the hurtful attitude or feeling that is in your right
   hand down on the floor.
5. Now hold the loving perspective in both hands and
   bring it to your heart. Imagine that perspective
   filling your heart and flooding your body.

4. What Is the Sacred Goodness in This Person that I Will See and Trust?

Created in the image of God, each person carries different, sacred attributes of God, such as wisdom, compassion, stead-fastness, joy, and creativity. Some people manifest this divine essence clearly; in others it is more hidden. Sometimes because of our natural attraction to a person, we see it easily. Other times differences, indifference, or active dislike prevents us from noticing it at all. Whether manifested or not, whether seen or not, something of God resides in each of us.

Looking for and seeing the goodness at the heart of another person cultivates a connection between us and that person. When we see a piece of God within a person, it builds appreciation in us and profoundly honors the other. When we are with another, love calls us to look for and become aware of the essential goodness of the person. What are we looking for? What are godlike aspects? Reflect on the comment, "Michael is really such a

> *As we are with another person, love calls us to look for and become aware of the essential goodness of the person.*

good person." Or, "Jennifer has a heart of gold." Let your mind move a level deeper to the attributes those stock phrases hint at. What is it that makes Michael a good person? His compassion? His steadfastness? What constitutes Jennifer's heart of gold? Her hospitality? Her trustworthiness? Simply being told we are a good person does not let us know we have been seen. It is nice to know that we are appreciated, but it is not the same as experiencing ourselves as being known.

Every Monday morning at 9 o'clock, Francis arrived at the office to enter the attendance information from worship. She faithfully went over every attendance slip and prayer request making sure that the information was correctly recorded and passed on to the appropriate person. She said little, but her spirit very much filled the office. This particular day pastor Sylvia walked into the office and was struck by the sense that Francis was doing holy work. It was as if she were watching an angel oversee the life of the congregation. Francis's heart for each name she recorded touched Sylvia deeply.

Once we have glimpsed a person's deep goodness, the next step is to trust it. That goodness is not a fleeting quality, but an essential part of that person. Whether we can see it regularly or not it lives in that individual. Trusting that it is there allows us to hold that holy goodness as an essential truth about the person, even when the person's words or behaviors may lead us to think otherwise. When we can stand in a loving place in relationship to someone and at the same time see the divinity within the person, the part of God within us joins with the part of God in that person. This establishes a holy connection between us.

The goodness we see in a person is not a fleeting quality, but an essential part of that person.

This next exercise will help you start to glimpse the holy goodness in others. Record reflections and thoughts in your journal.

Exercise 4.4

Seeing Someone's Goodness

Imagine you have been asked to speak at someone's memorial service. How would you answer the following questions?

- What qualities did you most admire?
- What impact did the person have on others and on you?
- What quality of God did the person display?

5. How Will I Acknowledge to a Person the Goodness I See in Him or Her?

We commonly offer positive words to people in response to their achievements. "Joey, what a great play you made in the fifth inning." Or, "Cindy, I really enjoyed your solo. You have a lovely voice." That kind of praise and appreciation communicates to the person that we like what we see or experience. And how important compliments, recognitions, and expressions of appreciation are! They are the lubricant that keeps relationships well oiled.

In addition to that type of positive interaction, loving relationships call for a deeper kind of acknowledgment. "Jake, your persistence made all the difference in this project." "Gloria, your courage rallied us all." "Josh, your tenderness shifted the tenor

Acknowledgments point to the traits that give rise to a person's words and actions.

of the entire meeting." Acknowledgments lift up essential qualities of a person. They point to the traits that give rise to a person's words and actions.

In society, we usually come closest to acknowledging the essence of people at funerals. In an attempt to honor a person, we work to say as clearly and accurately as we can what this person's life meant—what this man really stood for or what that woman uniquely brought into the world. Accomplishments are lifted up, but there is a concerted effort to catch the essence of who the person was. A great memorial service names the essence of a person with clarity and celebrates the difference that person made for us.

How often we have attended funerals and overheard people saying they wished the person could have heard what was said. Mary recently heard the comment, "Why don't we tell people these things when they're alive?" Sharing such personal acknowledgments creates an intimacy that can feel awkward even with people we know well. Funerals and memorial services create a space where such intimacy is acceptable, even fostered. We say the deeper things we are feeling as a way of honoring the person we loved who has died.

Love demands that we move past our awkwardness and honor the people we love while they live. Acknowledging who a person is, not just what they do, signals to them that we see past the exterior conditions of their life. We see and appreciate their very essence. Such witnessing creates deep connection and paves the way for love to flow more freely.

Exercise 4.5

Acknowledging to Others the Goodness We See in Them

Seeing the deeper goodness of another person may not come easily. The previous exercise offered ways to learn to see a person's goodness. This next exercise asks you to take a risk and express what you see.

1. Recall a person who you see regularly.
2. List three qualities of that person which you admire. Note them in your journal.
3. The next time you are with this person, specifically look for those qualities.
4. When you see that person demonstrating this quality, let the person know what you see.
5. Notice the impact on the other person and on you. Record your reflections.

6. What Will I Dare Ask of This Person?

Perhaps one of the most vulnerable things we can do is ask for what we really want from someone. The fear of looking weak or displaying a lack of self-sufficiency may keep us from requesting what we need and want. We may fear rejection, both of our request and ourselves. We may also fear how our request will impact the dynamics between us. Feeling imposed upon, will the person draw away? Or, having helped us, will they feel entitled to more than we can promise in return, leading us to draw away?

> *One of the most vulnerable things we can do is ask for what we really want from someone.*

Have you ever had an individual make a simple request and find yourself not only glad the person asked but actually feeling honored? Something happens in a relationship when requests are made. Requests signal that the other person places trust in us—a trust in our caring and goodness. Requests join people together in new and stronger ways.

Melissa's small group had met every other week for over a year. The members supported each other through prayer and caring listening when they met. Between their meetings, however, they really did not interact much with each other. Early on a Wednesday morning, Melissa received word that her father, who lived several states away, had suffered a severe stroke. She dropped everything and began making travel arrangements. Quickly becoming overwhelmed with the details, she sent an e-mail to the members of her small group. In it, she gave them the time of her flight and asked them to arrange among themselves some way of getting her to the airport. She quickly received reassurance that they would arrange her transportation and contact her later with the details.

Independent and self-sufficient, making this request was out of character for Melissa. Her group members were surprised and honored that in a moment of crisis she turned to them for help. Her request allowed them not just to see her life, but to be part of it. Melissa had always appreciated the support expressed by these women. Now she experienced that care and support in a concrete way. Their quick response touched her heart.

Requests invite others to be a part of our lives.

Melissa's request reflected a true need. She communicated in a way that was clear and that she knew would be heard. Knowing the circumstances of her group members, she knew that between them and people they knew, they would be able to help her.

Loving requests are not outlandish. They do not set up someone else for failure; rather, they acknowledge the other person's freedom to say no. Loving requests come from our recognition of what we need and what another person can provide. Requests are clear, honest expressions of what we want from a person. They recognize and value the strengths a person possesses. Requests give others the opportunity to make a contribution to us and to our relationship.

For many, requests are hard to make. The fear of indebtedness may block us from asking for what we want and need. More important than any indebtedness we might incur is the important acknowledgment that we need each other. In the end, we cannot find personal fulfillment and effectiveness apart from others.

The kindom of God is like a grand ecological system. Life is interdependent. The well-being of one part depends on the well-being of all the other parts. Daring to ask another person for something embodies our interdependence. Daring to ask and opening ourselves to receiving takes us one step further into affirming our connectedness and experiencing the kindom of God.

Exercise 4.6

Making Requests

1. As you are in conversation with someone this week, notice if there is something you want or need from that person which you have never dared ask for before. For example, prayer for a particular situation, lending a helping hand with a project, or providing a listening ear.

2. Ask that person for what you need.
3. Afterwards, reflect on what the experience was like. What made it easy or difficult? What was the impact both on you and the other person? Record personal experiences in your journal.

A Concluding Story

Pastor George received word he was being assigned a new supervisor. His heart sank when he learned it was Janet. Janet had preceded him as pastor in his previous congregation and George's tenure in that congregation had not gone well. Attendance dropped, tension increased, and congregants continually criticized him for not measuring up to Janet. George ended his time at that congregation under clouded conditions. He left feeling like a failure. George heard through the grapevine that Janet had commented, "I sure wish they'd appointed a competent pastor to follow me."

Now in a different congregation, George's gifts matched well the needs of the congregation. The people felt he provided strong and caring leadership. Things had been going so well, and now this. George had grave concerns about Janet becoming his supervisor. He disliked her and distrusted her ability to see what he brought in this new setting. "Not one day of supervising me and I'm sure she's already made up her mind about me. She'll never be fair."

Thinking about working under conditions like that made him sick. He longed for a relationship with his supervisor marked by mutual respect and trust. It dawned on George that this meant he would have to respect and trust her too. George began to reflect on what it would require of him to respect and trust Janet. He would have to adopt an attitude of openness to the gifts she brought to the position and to giving her a chance.

George knew that to do that, he would have to let go of some things. He needed to find a way to set aside his feelings of shame about his last pastorate. He also needed to find a way to set aside his anger around the comment that had been attributed to Janet. George began praying for the ability to see Janet in a new light.

After working on this for several months, George found himself developing a beginning appreciation for her expertise, wisdom, and straightforwardness. During a supervisory meeting, George acknowledged the difference her expertise was making in their region. He learned to appreciate her bluntness—he never had to guess what she was thinking—and he told her that.

The hardest challenge for George was the day he called her to ask for advice on an issue in the congregation. He found he had to walk back through all the choices he had made previously. He had to remind himself of what was truly important to him and the attitudes he wanted to embody. He found he once again had to set aside feelings of shame about his performance at his previous congregation.

A year later George and Janet had a relationship marked by respect and openness. Much room for growth remained, but it was light years from the horror George had thought inevitable.

We have the power to shift what our relationship with another person is like. Our choices influence the nature of our relationships. What dreams do we choose to feed? What perspectives do we choose to hold? Which grudges or hurts will we set aside? What qualities will we choose to look for and acknowledge in another person? What will we dare ask of them? Making these choices may not be easy. They are, however, the way we can begin to right our relationships and experience what God has in mind for those relationships.

We have the power to shift what our relationship with another person is like.

Chapter

Five | Forming and Living
the Relationship

U p until this point, we have been preparing
ourselves to be in right relationship by
building skills in self-awareness, self-management, and social
awareness. Self-awareness provides insight and understanding about the expectations and emotions we bring to encounters with others. Well-developed self-management muscles
allow us to manage our attitudes and emotions, freeing us
from blind, involuntary reactions and giving us the power of
choice. Social awareness moves us beyond our assumptions
and biases to see in the fullest way possible the person we
are with. That helps us develop an appreciation of who they
are and their essential goodness, and opens further the way
for right relationship.

We turn a corner with this chapter. We move from focusing
on ourselves or on the other person or persons to looking at
the relationship between us. How
we conduct our relationships determines the degree of fulfillment and
effectiveness in our life and work. A

> *A right relationship provides
> an open channel through
> which God can work.*

right relationship is a foretaste of the kindom of God. It provides a channel for God to work through on earth.

Certain structural components supply guidance and support as people work collectively to help God's dreaming find
form in the world. Right relationships help people align

themselves for a common task. They allow people the freedom to design their relationship for maximum satisfaction and productivity. Right relationships anchor a group in the presence, power, and vision of God. This chapter focuses on how a group can build and live a right relationship.

Three Structural Components

Self-awareness, self-management, and social awareness provide the foundational skills for right relationship. These foundational skills allow us to connect authentically and creatively with others. The addition of three components creates a strong and flexible structure that helps a relationship fulfill its God-given purpose. The three components are (1) finding alignment around our task, (2) developing covenant agreements about how we want life together to be like and how to achieve that, and (3) opening ourselves to what God is attempting to birth through us as a group.

The three structural components of right relationship are:

1. *Finding alignment around our task*
2. *Developing covenant agreements about how we will live and work together*
3. *Opening ourselves to God's Spirit*

Alignment helps groups develop and hold a common understanding of their task and goals. The work of finding alignment surfaces the interests and values of the members of the group so they can determine which ones will guide their work. Covenant agreements allow participants to custom design a relationship, creating a satisfying way of living and working together. Covenant agreements establish safety, helping us know what we can expect from each other. Openness to God helps us hear how God wants to use us. It attunes our dreaming to the dreaming of God. Though groups can deal with these components in any order, all three must be addressed.

Finding Alignment

"I get so frustrated in these meetings," George muttered. "All we've done so far is talk. It's time to stop talking and do something!" Cheryl looked at him, "Sure, but what exactly are we supposed to do?" And so began the fourth meeting of the building task force at Canyon Creek congregation. Silence prevailed, until Jack turned to the chair and said with quiet force, "I thought we were charged with bringing back a recommendation about expanding the facility. I feel like you've manipulated and stretched that into all kinds of other things to suit your purpose." Stan, the chairperson of the task force, sputtered, "But you were the one who said we needed to have a bigger vision in order to know how to proceed!" The group spent the next hour searching for a way out of the mire. George lobbied for action, Cheryl for prayer and discernment, Jack for visioning. As the meeting progressed, camps arose around each of those areas. Tension and anxiety increased as movement forward seemed more and more impossible to them.

That is what happens when a group does not have alignment around their task and goals. Alignment helps a group develop and hold a common understanding of the work they face and the outcomes they desire. The work of alignment clarifies which interests and values will direct their work. The process of reaching alignment turns a room

> Alignment helps a group develop and hold a common understanding of the work they face and the outcomes they desire.

of individuals with multiple understandings of their work into a team with a common focus. In an aligned group each person is committed to something bigger than themselves and their own interests.

Although work on alignment is particularly vital when a group faces a new task, that work must be continued throughout the duration of the task. Anytime a group feels stuck or at loggerheads, taking the time to check alignment is a wise idea. It may indicate that group members are focused on their own personal issues rather than on the bigger issue at hand. This can lead them to wrestling with each other instead of wrestling together with the problem. In those instances, returning the group's focus to the task and desired outcome can help get them back on track. There are two primary alignment tasks:

1. Putting the issue out front and clarifying it.
2. Identifying the interests and values that will guide their work.

Put the Issue Out Front and Clarify It

For a group to be effective in their work and find fulfillment in it, group members need clarity around their task and the outcomes they desire. A clear understanding of their work aligns a group's thinking and focuses their energy.

The building task force at Canyon Creek gathered the following week in the conference room. Stan, the chairperson of the task force, was relieved to see people had returned. The last meeting had ended with people feeling tremendously frustrated. As the meeting started off, Sally, one of the quieter members of the team, suggested a possibility. "I don't know if this would be helpful for us or not. But my work team at the office does something each time we start a project to help us get on the same page. We used to get really frustrated with each other and this has helped us."

Stan looked to the other members of the group, who shrugged and nodded. George said, "Might as well. It certainly can't make things worse." Sally went on to say, "First, we try and figure out what our job is. I got to thinking that maybe part of our problem is that we each have a different understanding of what this team is supposed to be doing"

"Oh, I don't think so," said Stan. "That's clear. We're here to discern the vision for our facility." Julia heaved a big sigh and Frank crossed his legs and turned sideways. The room was silent. "What?" said Stan. "Isn't that why we're here?" Jack looked at him and said, "That may be clear to you, but it's certainly not clear to me." Samuel agreed, "I know we're called the building task force, but are we to assess the current building and recommend how to renovate what's here? Or, can we look at moving the facility into that area of new development." "And where does our job end?" asked Julia. "Do we just bring recommendations or are we supposed to then lead the building project itself? What does the congregation expect from us?" Stan turned to Sally and said, "Looks like your idea might be just what we need to do."

The team spent the rest of the evening and the entirety of the next meeting addressing their purpose. They wrote in large letters on a piece of newsprint the name of their team, "Building Task Force" and under that the words, "What's our task?" They displayed the newsprint on the wall and turned their chairs to face it. Stan distributed copies of the minutes from the board meeting where the task force was created. They read through the minutes to determine the board's intent for them and then discussed their understanding of that intent.

As insights came about their purpose and task, they posted them on the wall surrounding the original piece of newsprint. Somehow having them up on the wall changed the dynamics in the group. People saw that their comments were not getting lost and they let go of having to defend them quite so vigorously. Seeing them up there also helped them realize how differently they understood their task. They knew that in order to move ahead, they had to reach a common understanding.

> *Having comments posted on the wall changed the dynamics in the group. People saw that their ideas were not getting lost and they let go of having to defend them quite so vigorously.*

At the next meeting, the group again gathered around the displayed newsprint. "What's really important about all this?" asked Stan as he gestured to the wall. "What can we agree on as our fundamental task?" This time it seemed easier and by the end of the meeting the team had come to agreement about their job. As they sat there in their closing time, there was a new spirit in the room. For the first time, they felt like a team.

The group at Canyon Creek took three important steps in finding clarity about their task. First, they discussed the issue of their task and put it in front of them where all could see. In their case the issue was, "What is the task of our team?" An established staffing group might decide their issues is, "What is the task of our team as regards hiring the music director?" A finance committee might lift as their issue, "What is the task of our team regarding the financial crisis we're facing?" By writing down the task-related question and displaying it for the group to see, the question does not get lost, but focuses the discussion. People physically turn as a group to face it. That was the moment the group at Canyon Creek first began to find cohesiveness. They now had their first agreed-upon task. Together, they would seek to answer the question, "What is the task of our team?"

The second important step the task force took was surfacing information about their task. This meant familiarizing themselves with the directives given to them by the board that formed them. It also meant identifying what each person in the group understood those directives to mean. The Canyon Creek team captured people's comments and placed them on the wall along with the initial question. This reassured the members of the team that their comments were being heard and considered. With all of the information on the wall, the team could stand back and together look at the whole of it. This visual depiction helps a group see the commonalities and divergences of thinking. They begin to sense what could be the commonly held understanding of the group.

The third step was continuing to talk and listen until they came to a common understanding of their task. Sometimes this step takes time. Some groups will find alignment around their task very quickly; others will struggle. Giving this step the time it needs results in groups that work more efficiently and effectively. Knowing exactly what their job is, helps to clearly define what their job is not. When a group does not have clarity around their task, group members experience frustration and a lack of satisfying movement. They spend their energy mired in side issues or on work that belongs to somebody else.

The Canyon Creek team was a newly formed group; however, this work applies to long-established groups as well. A committee that has existed for many years may know precisely what their purpose is. But, as they deal with each new issue or project that comes their way, they must answer the question, "What is our task regarding this issue?"

Exercise 5.1

Clarifying the Focus of Your Work

1. What is the issue your group is facing? It may be a task, a problem, or a challenge. Quickly sum it up in no more than 10 words and write it in large letters on a piece of newsprint. (Some examples include addressing adult leadership for the senior high youth, fixing the roof, recruiting teachers for the education program, planning the women's retreat, grounds maintenance during the summer, and so on. Do not be surprised if there is some fuzziness in naming it.)

2. Hang the newsprint on the wall. Now physically turn your chairs (or stand) so that everyone is facing the task on the wall.

3. Begin to surface participant's understandings of the task and of your group's responsibilities regarding it. As comments are made, summarize them and place them on the wall along with the original. Check with each speaker to make sure that the words or words used to summarize their comments accurately capture them. Use the following questions to help guide your discussion:

   - Is there a mandate given to us by another group? If so, what is it? What do we each think that means?
   - What is each participant's understanding of the task?
   - What does this task involve?
   - Who does it involve?
   - Is this task ongoing or are there deadlines associated with it?
   - What is this group's specific role regarding it?
   - How will we know when our task is complete?
   - What is unclear to us about our task?

4. Look at what is on the wall. Talk about what you see and look for how things fit together. Group comments by common themes. What are the common threads that you see? What on the wall is helpful, and even important, but not the central part of your work? Continue to discuss until the group reaches consensus on the primary focus of your work.

5. Summarize the task in written form. At subsequent meetings, either post it on the wall or have it available in printed form as you work on that task.

Identify Interests and Values

With clarity about their focus, the building task force at Canyon Creek began work. It soon became clear that each person brought different interests. Mike lived across the street and had strong opinions about the design of the parking lot. Alice, the mother of teenagers, continually raised the question of how proposed building changes would help or hurt the youth program. George, a long-time choir member, wanted to see improvements in the acoustics of the sanctuary. They could count on Hilda to steer any conversation back to maintenance and upkeep concerns.

Along with the interests that arose, different values surfaced. Sally remarked, "I think it's really important we communicate clearly and often with the congregation and get input from them." "I think that's true," offered Henry, "but it's far more important that we meet our deadlines." Instantly the team polarized into two groups, debating the wisdom of one against the other. "Time out!" Stan interjected into the conversation. "I'm hearing two important values being lifted up: open communication and meeting deadlines. It may well be that both need to be honored. I'm wondering if there are other values we want to honor as well. Now would be a good time to talk about the interests and values we each have. We are each attached to different aspects of the project. It would be good to name those things."

Nodding at the wisdom of this, the team agreed to spend some time identifying the interests and values that people brought to the task. Alice asked for a definition of the word *interest.* Stan answered, "An interest is the investment a person has in the project or the outcome." They first listed the interests that had already surfaced, and displayed that list on newsprint for everyone to see. They include Mike's investment in

> *An interest is the investment a person has in the project or the outcome.*

adequate parking and Alice's investment that their proposal be supportive or at least not hindering of youth ministry. They made sure each person's personal interests got recorded on the wall.

On a separate piece of newsprint labeled "Canyon Creek," the group members recorded what they knew of the congregation's interests. They reviewed the congregation's mission and vision statement and from that pulled out four key interests. Also, an additional sheet of newsprint was labeled "God." They dreamed what God's interests might be. "What," they asked themselves, "is God's investment in this? What might God want to be accomplishing through the renovation of our facility?"

Together, they looked at the wall of interests in front of them: their own personal ones, the congregation's, and God's. They asked themselves, "Which of these interests will we give priority to, allowing them to guide us in our decisions?" As they talked, it became clear to them that certain interests were primary. They agreed that these would guide their work and recommendations. Other interests they acknowledged as important but not primary. They would honor those as they could.

They then looked at values. "Now, what do you mean by values?" asked Alice again. Stan replied, "Values are the principles and standards for living that are foundationally important to us." "Oh," said Alice, "you mean like harmony as we do our work?" "Exactly," said Stan. "Let's start getting these up on newsprint." Using the same process they utilized to identify interests, they surfaced their personal values. "What are our values as we think about this project and our working together on it?"

After eliciting personal values, they added a piece of newsprint and listed the values of the congregation. Then, they added a third piece of newsprint, and imagined what God's values might be for their project and their working together on it. When the lists were complete, they stood back and together looked at them all. Talking over the values listed, five emerged as foundational values that all agreed would be honored: respect for each person's voice, respect for the earth and its resources, open and honest communication, honoring commitments, playfulness and good humor.

Identifying interests and values takes both time and energy, but the benefits far outweigh the cost. Agreed-upon and commonly held interests guide the group to work towards specific outcomes. Values provide an agreed upon set of principles and standards for their work together. The following exercise is the step-by-step process used by the Canyon Creek task force in the story above.

Values provide an agreed upon set of principles and standards for a group's work.

Exercise 5.2

Identifying Our Interests and Values

IDENTIFYING INTERESTS

1. Allow 60 seconds of silence for each person to reflect on why the task is personally important to them. Have them reflect on the following:

   • How does this affect you?
   • What is your investment in this?
   • What's really important to you about this?

   Share your reflections with each other. Speak as honestly as you can and listen deeply to the others. You do not have to agree, simply seek to understand what it is like for the other people in the group.

   As comments are offered, summarize them on newsprint. Check with each speaker to make sure that the words used to summarize speakers' comments accurately capture them.

2. Allow 60 seconds of silence for each person to reflect on the interests of the larger congregation.

   • What is the importance of this issue for the well-being of our congregation?
   • What impact will our decisions have on the congregation's mission and ministry?

   Share your reflections with each other. Speak as honestly as you can and listen deeply to others. Capture comments on another sheet of newsprint labeled "Our Congregation."

   If your congregation has a mission or vision statement, review it. What does it say about the congregation's investment in the issue your group faces?

3. Allow 60 seconds of silence for each person to reflect on the interests of God. Ask the following questions:

   • What is God's investment in our task?
   • What is important to God about this?

   Share your reflections with each other and capture comments on a third piece of newsprint labeled "God."

4. Together, look at all of the interests that now hang before you on the wall. Ask the following questions and record responses on newsprint:

   • Which of these interests will we give priority to, allowing them to guide our decisions?
   • Which of these remaining interests will we hold as important though not primary?

5. At subsequent meetings, post the list of primary and secondary interests or have them available in print to help guide your work and decision making.

IDENTIFYING VALUES
Using the same basic process found in the first part of this exercise, now surface the values (principles and standards) that will guide your group. (Values might

include respect, open communication, audacity, harmony, collaboration, courage, aliveness, forgiveness, inclusivity, authenticity, caring, creativity, boldness, etc.) As comments are made, summarize them on newsprint for all to see.

1. Allow 60 seconds of silence for each person to reflect on the values each would like to see guide the group's work, and then share your reflections.
2. Allow 60 seconds of silence for each person to reflect on the values embodied by the larger congregation. What congregational values might be important for us to honor? Share your reflections and note them on newsprint.
3. Allow 60 seconds of silence for each person to reflect on God's values. What are the principles and standards God might say are important for us to honor? Share and record the answers.
4. Together, look at all of the values that now hang before you on the wall. Ask the following questions and record responses on newsprint:

   • Which of these values will we give priority to, allowing them to guide our decisions?
   • Which of these remaining values will we hold as important though not primary?

5. At subsequent meetings, post the list of primary and secondary values or have them available in print to help guide your work and decision making.

Developing Covenant Agreements

How shall we work together, specifically? What are our expectations around attendance at meetings? How shall we communicate outside of meetings? How do we want to deal with disagreement or conflict? How do we want our meetings to feel? What do we need to do in order in ensure that? Covenant agreements allow a group to design its relationship so that it honors the group's interests and embodies the group's values. Covenant agreements specify how a group will work together. They define what each participant can count on from the other.

Covenant agreements help build dependable and trusting relationships—they can be made at any time in a group's life. New groups will want to design their agreements early in their life together. Existing groups will find addressing covenant agreements especially helpful when they are experiencing dis-ease or conflict. Revisiting expectations and clarifying the group's rules of conduct provide safety and stability in such times. Some groups choose to create a covenant before they do anything else. Basic ground rules are essential. But we think that more specific covenant agreements are more easily and precisely made when a group is centered on what they are trying to achieve and the principles and standards of behavior they want to honor.

> *Covenant agreements allow a group to specify how it will work together and define what each can count on from the other.*

The building task force at Canyon Creek now knew their task, and a list of the major interests that would guide their work displayed on the wall. Next to it was a list of the primary values they would honor as they worked together.

At their next meeting, however, they had run into trouble. An e-mail sharing a piece of information had gone out to some, but not to all, causing confusion. The group had depended on having information George had agreed to bring from the city planning office. George, however, arrived without it. And as if that were not enough, Cheryl was absent for the second meeting in a row and no one had heard from her. The meeting had felt tense and awkward. People were upset with each other, but did not know how to express it or even if they had a right to express it. At the end of the meeting, they went through their usual ritual of going over what went well and what could have gone better. Out of that discussion, they decided they needed to take time at their next meeting to develop agreements about what they could expect from each other.

The following week they gathered in their meeting space. Hanging on the wall were lists of the interests and values that would guide them. Stan was the first to speak: "At our last meeting, we agreed that we wanted our work to be both effective for the congregation and fulfilling for each one of us. We also agreed that our work at the last meeting was neither. So as you look at what we're committed to, what agreements do we need to make around how we work with each other?"

Once they started speaking, the discussion was fairly brief. Attendance at all meetings was expected. Unforeseen emergencies would, of course, arise, but barring those, people were expected to be there. Group members would only accept tasks they knew they could complete on time. In order to keep everyone informed, they would copy the entire group on all e-mails. Group members would speak the full truth of what was on their heart and mind here in the group, rather that in sidebar conversations outside. They would look for the wisdom of God in each person's comment. The team summed up the covenant agreements and printed them on newsprint and hung the new list on the wall. At each meeting the three lists (interests, values, and agreements) would remind them of what they worked towards and how they would do it.

These covenant agreements provided the group at Canyon Creek with the structure they needed to work effectively. Each group's agreements will be different. They arise out of the unique circumstances of the group, the values they wish to embody, and the outcomes they are trying to achieve. The personalities of the participants, and the group itself, make a difference. For example, covenant agreements can be made around the question,

Covenant agreements arise out of the unique circumstances of the group, the values they wish to embody, and the outcomes they are trying to achieve.

"How do we want to be with each other when we disagree?" Some groups agree ahead of time that ranting and raving is perfectly acceptable as long as people do not blame or show contempt. Others design ways that honor their preference for quieter ways of managing conflict.

By placing their covenant agreements on the wall, the Canyon Creek team invited and empowered the group members to hold the group accountable for what they had together committed to. Having the agreements visible gives group members the permission to point to them at any time and call the group back to its commitments. Covenant agreements are powerful tools, but only to the extent that the group actually uses them.

Exercise 5.3

Developing Covenant Agreements

1. If your group has completed exercises 5.1 and 5.2, post the results—the understanding of your task, and the interests and values that will guide your work—where people can see them.

2. As a group, reflect on what would help make your work both effective and fulfilling. What agreements does your group need to make around how you will work with each other? Be sure to include things like the group's expectations of the following:

   - Attendance
   - Confidentiality
   - How meetings are set
   - How information is shared
   - Starting and stopping times
   - How the group will handle conflict
   - How the group will celebrate success
   - How the group will handle individual or group failure

Opening Ourselves to God's Spirit

The work we do in our congregations seeks to open a channel for God to be present with power in the world. This necessitates that we make enough space for God to be present. Clarity about our task, our interests, and our values; convenantal agreements that provide the ground rules for our conduct—together they create an important structure that help us work efficiently and effectively. If we are not careful, however, that structure can become a house without doors or windows in which we find ourselves trapped. For our groups to find and embody the creativity, liveliness, and Spirit that they seek, we must make space for God's Spirit.

Life and work had smoothed out for the building task force at Canyon Creek. People knew what they were there to do and knew what they could count on from each other, providing order and predictability. One evening as they sat around their meeting table, Cheryl said, "I'm starting to hate those pieces of paper on the wall." People looked at her with surprise. "They felt good at the beginning, but now I see them and feel constrained, like I can't breathe." The room was quiet. "I don't know," said Jack. "I always breathe a bit easier when I walk in and see them on the wall."

The work we do in our congregations seeks to open a channel for God to be present with power in the world.

"I think Cheryl may be on to something," said Sally. Gesturing to the newsprint, she added, "These lists outlining our task, the interests we're working towards, and our behavioral agreements structure our work—and we really need that. Order is good, but not at the expense of creativity. I don't think we've left much room for Spirit."

"Wow," said Mike sighing deeply. "You're right. I can feel my body relaxing even as you say it. We've gotten pretty rigid, haven't we?" "Those lists are important," George interjected forcefully. "They've ensured our efficiency." Glaring at Stan, he added, "Don't even think about taking them down." "I wasn't," said Stan. "They're a great help to us. I was just wondering how we might open up some other space. Not literally, of course. But is there some way of inviting a bit more of the Spirit's playful, chaotic, creativeness into our work?"

"Chaos!" boomed George. "We've spent two months trying to get rid of chaos!" "Exactly!" said Jack. "And as a result, we're orderly and efficient . . . and bored. When was the last time you were excited about coming to one of our meetings? When was the last time our meetings were animated and energizing?" The room again grew quiet. Even George was silent. Hal spoke, "In the beginning, when the earth was a formless void . . . God created. It's in the chaos that God creates." Stan said softly, "So, how do we create a space for God's chaos here?"

As the group talked further, they all agreed that the controls and guides they had created for themselves were important and helpful tools. They also agreed that the purpose of those tools was to help them be a more effective channel for God to work through. They existed to help keep the channel open, not to close it down. They brainstormed a variety of ways to help open some space for God. In the end, the Canyon Creek group decided on three things to help make more space for God's Spirit.

First, they arranged tables so there was an open space in their midst. This open space, encircled by the people and their commitments that hung on the wall, created a visual symbol of being a channel for God's Spirit. It would help them welcome and support the surprises the Spirit would bring.

Second, the group would use the open space as a focus for their opening and closing times. Knowing it was easy for them to forget, they wanted to remind themselves at the beginning of each meeting, that whatever their plans might be, their job was to birth God's plans. At the end of the meeting, the space would remind them to reflect on how God had been present, working through them that evening.

Third, in the midst of a meeting, they would use that space to call them back to God's Spirit. Each person could point to the space at anytime and call a time out, inviting the group to ask themselves questions such as, "What is God trying to do through us right now? What does Spirit have to say to us? What is God's perspective on this?" They added to their covenant agreements that any person at any time could call for that kind of reflection by the group.

The Canyon Creek team created the structures that worked for them to welcome God's Spirit. Each group will find its own ways, but three points in particular help a group to remain open to God's Spirit. A visual cue of some kind continually reminds a group that God is present. It also reminds them of their commitment to be aware and responsive. Opening rituals anchor a group in an anticipatory perspective. Closing

> *Inviting and welcoming God's Spirit increases both energy and unpredictability.*

rituals help the group find the greater meaning in their work and time together. A permission-giving structure, such as the team's time out, places the responsibility in the hands of team members. It asks and empowers each person to call the group back to being a channel for God's creative work.

The Canyon Creek team found, as other teams do, that inviting God into their midst increased both energy and unpredictability. Life was not as smooth and tidy, and sometimes they argued. They also found that they laughed more and were struck by moments of awe. They began to see their work as God's work.

Exercise 5.4

Opening Yourselves to Spirit

As a group, discuss the following:

1. Our scriptures are full of stories of how God's Spirit has worked through individuals and groups. Imagine the story of your group being a story of God's Spirit working through a group.

   • How did your story begin?
   • How did God bring you together?
   • What happened next?
   • What's the name and the theme of this chapter of your story?
   • Look ahead. What do you imagine happens next in your story?
   • What do you imagine the twists and turns will be?
   • How do you imagine it ending?
   • Looking now at the whole of the story, what was God trying to achieve in the world through your group?

2. Look back over the preceding section where the Canyon Creek team creates structures to help them remain open to God's Spirit. Note what they create visually and ritually and the way they put power in the hands of team members to call the group to accountability.

- What structures does your team already have in place that open, keep you open, or reopen you to God's presence and creative power?
- What structures does your team want to add?

Continuing to Live the Relationship

The difficult part is not so much forming right relationships as living them. The shifts and changes in our relationships require that we shift and change as well. The discipline of right relationship requires self-awareness and self-management. It requires our awareness of and ability to see and hear the people we are with. It calls for an ongoing openness to God and the movement of Spirit. It calls us to choose continually to live out love. It means hanging in there physically, emotionally, and spiritually, when it would seem easier or more appealing to walk away.

> *The difficult part is not so much forming right relationships as living them.*

The Canyon Creek team met nearly every week for the next seven months. Across that time they discovered something about their relationship. It changed. And, it changed not once, but many times. Just when they thought their work had settled into smooth and predictable patterns, circumstances would arise to disrupt those patterns. The congregation's board gave additional responsibilities to the building task force. The city changed zoning rules, blocking one path the team had been pursuing. Each time outside circumstances changed, the team had to realign themselves, revisiting their task and goals

Just when they thought they knew what to expect from each other, people on the team seemed to change. Life circumstances affected the ability of some to be fully present in spirit as well as body at their meetings. Hilda's father came to live with her. Evenings were difficult for him and she often had to stay at home to comfort him. Frank went through a divorce. And while he was physically present at every meeting, his moods were unpredictable. Every so often the team would change or add a covenant agreement to reflect the changes happening beyond and within their group.

At one meeting, a number of the members came close to resigning. A disagreement over a seemingly insignificant item blew up into a full-blown argument. The meeting ended with participants angry but committed to stay together. When the team met the following week, they looked at each other and, to their surprise, started laughing. "What in the world was that all about?" they asked both themselves and God's Spirit. That led to many subsequent discussions about conflict—how scary it was for them and yet how at times it might actually serve them.

As time went on, the group became more comfortable with conflict. They learned that conflict often brought forth new ideas or surfaced important but unexpressed thoughts and feelings. They discovered they could increase their sense of safety and their ability to remain in tension by utilizing the structures they had created for themselves. Revisiting their agreements around which interests and values they would honor, and their agreements for how to conduct themselves, held them steady.

The team came to realize that their main trap was a preference for order. They loved their lists and loved working efficiently. Things would be going comfortably and then slowly, slowly, the energy in the group would go down. Someone would finally notice that the group had lost their spark and spirit. They learned that loss of spark and spirit indicated that they had once again shut out God's Spirit. Each time they made new space for Spirit, energy and enthusiasm for their work returned. It renewed their understanding of the meaning and importance of their work.

Circumstances continually change. The relationship provides an open channel for God's work in the world as a group remains responsive and flexible. We maintain flexibility by revisiting alignment around task, adjusting covenant agreements, and opening ourselves to God's creative Spirit.

Chapter |
Six | Troubleshooting

Questions and Answers

L iving right relationship happens in real circumstances. The following questions are from people working to create or maintain creative, mutual, and generative relationships in their own settings. These responses suggest ways of using the principles of right relationship to find the answers to your own questions.

Q. *I know people need to be heard, but I also know progress can be slowed by talk, talk, talk. How important is the talk?*

A. Some talk serves a crucial purpose; some does not. Conversation can move a group toward greater productivity or steer them away from it. It can even serve as a work avoidance strategy. In a work group, both task and relationship must be tended to for the group to engage in creative, effective, and satisfying work. Failure to spend adequate time sharing thoughts and feelings will impede the progress they want to make.

Groups are well served by taking time to honor "deep democracy"—letting every voice have its say. Deep democracy says the reality of a situation is not fully heard until each person has shared his perspective. Each perspective, however limited, sees an aspect missed by other perspectives. All are needed for the group to move ahead with wisdom.

Deep democracy begins with individuals listening to themselves. Each of us has multiple internal voices that hold opinions on issues. Rarely do the words we speak on a topic reflect the complexity of our thoughts and feelings about it. We sift through the voices, sorting them into the ones we think are appropriate to share in that setting. For instance, a volunteer in the office brings her two-year-old with her when she comes to help. When the secretary was asked if that was okay, she said of course, and meant it; that is, about 92 percent. There was also 6 percent of her that wanted to suggest that the woman leave the child with her grandmother, and 2 percent that wanted to scream, "What, are you crazy? That's just what we need around here—more chaos!"

In a heartbeat, the secretary sifted through her inner thoughts and feelings and arrived at her answer to the woman, sharing the dominant voice. But, if she was not aware of that other 8 percent, it might well pop out of her mouth on a stressful day, surprising her as well as others.

We often judge those smaller inner voices, saying one is good, another bad, one is right, another wrong. We may want to ignore some or even silence them. But each of these inner voices has some wisdom to add as we reflect on an issue. Ignoring the voices we judge as wrong may mean that we fail to listen to an interest or value that really does need to be heard. Aware of that other 8 percent, the secretary added to her response, "Now, let's strategize about what to do on those days when the office gets crazy." She chose not to share the eye-rolling, hair-pulling "What, are you crazy?" voice. But she recognized that it lifted up something that needed to be taken into consideration—not adding more chaos on chaotic days. Because she listened for the underlying message of it, she heard the wisdom it brought. As a result, she designed agreements with the volunteer that honored both the volunteer's needs and hers.

The same is true for groups. Each individual carries a piece of wisdom needed by the team. Some voices will fill the room with eloquence and clear wisdom. Some will be tentative and flow haltingly from a person's mouth. Some people will speak calmly and rationally, while others will rant and rave. Some will express a perspective that the group may want to quietly ignore or aggressively beat down. Each voice, however, carries information the group needs in order to make wise choices.

As with an individual, the silenced or unheard voice in a group will eventually find expression—and often in unhelpful or even harmful ways. The ignored or marginalized voice may manifest itself as the disenchantment and withdrawal of a person from the group or through passive or active undermining of the group's work. Thoughts and feelings not shared within the group often get shared on the telephone or in the parking lot with others. Encouraging participants to share not just their dominant feelings with the group, but the nagging 2 percent voices as well, ultimately serves the group and its mission.

Q. *My problem is not with a group, but one person with whom I work. I chair a committee and I like the new pastor well enough, but she has a habit of dropping projects on me that need immediate attention. They're good ideas, but we never have the time to do them as well as we'd like and it wreaks havoc with our other projects. I'm starting to feel a bit resentful.*

A. The processes we outline for groups in chapter 5 apply to two-person relationships as well. Everything we have groups doing can be helpful for partnerships.

This sounds like an instance where it would be helpful for the two of you to develop some covenant agreements around how work is assigned. Relationships so often develop just the way you are describing. Two people begin working together, each bringing with them expectations and preferred ways of working, as well as other patterns learned in other settings.

Fortunately, we do not have to hang onto patterns if they are not working. Colleagues can design between them how they will work, so that the gifts and needs of both are honored. Sit down with your new pastor and discuss goals for her helping the group do its established work well, as well as discussing how to approach new projects. Let her know that the pattern you two have fallen into makes both of those goals difficult to accomplish, and that you are feeling frustrated. Get curious about her goals for the work of your group and the church. Talk about how you both would like your work together to feel. (Efficient? Relaxed? Creative? Friendly?) Together, design how work needs to flow between the two of you to accomplish all that. People cannot read our minds, so making clear requests helps both them and us. Exercises 5.1, 5.2, and 5.3 can be helpful for structuring your conversations.

People cannot really know the impact their actions have on us unless we tell them. When we make a request, it informs the other person about what we want or need from them. Our request puts both them and us more at choice, affirming that we both have power in the relationship. We have the power to ask for what we want. They have the power to say yes or no, or make a counteroffer or request, suggesting an alternative.

Q. *I've been part of two or three truly terrific groups, so I've got a great model for how relationships should be. This group I'm in now is so different. How do I help it be more like the other ones?*

A. We hear your desire to have more of your really great past experiences. Because the history of a group, personalities of participants, and tasks of the group differ, every group differs. Really great groups have one thing in common, however: right relationship. With right relationship in a group, honor, respect, love, and care characterize the way people interact regardless of history, personalities, or tasks.

Having experienced right relationship in your other groups, you bring a tremendous gift to the new group. You know what relationships can be like. You have a high dream for your new group. Your greatest hopes and dreams for your group serve you and your group well. Bring your skills of social awareness (chapter 3) and skills of how to love (chap-

ter 4) into the group. Settle for nothing less than being a cata-
lyst for the transformation of the group.

Even when your new group does embody right relationships, your new setting will require you to shift. We remember two different staffing committees in congregations we
worked with. One, situated in a farming community, was
rather slow-moving and folksy. The other, in the downtown
area of a large city, was focused and business-like, and argued often and loudly. In both groups, relationships demonstrated the characteristics of right relationship. Right
relationship guided the work of both.

Shock hardly describes experiencing moving from membership in one to membership in the other. With right relationship present in both groups, the change, however
shocking, can be a gift. Groups can be transformed by a new
person. And a new group can be a transformational opportunity for the person new to it.

New situations challenge a person to explore and develop
new parts of himself. How do I, who am comfortable with
"slow-moving and folksy," learn to live with "focused and
business-like"? One is not right and the other wrong; one not
good and the other bad. Each is simply a different form of
living in right relationship. The unfamiliar form challenges
me to discover and develop an additional part of myself. The
challenge gives me the opportunity to step more fully into
the full range of who I am. And with right relationships found
in both settings, I enjoy the safety of daring to step into new
ways of behaving and living.

Enjoy your new group. Bring the gift of yourself into the
group. Allow the group to bring the gift of itself into your life.

Q. *The same folks seem always to get asked to fill leadership
roles. I'm continually asked to chair committees. It's flatter-
ing, I suppose, but I'm really tired of it. I'd like to just be a
regular member of one.*

A. It sounds like you may be suffering from what is called
"role nausea," which is when we get sick and tired of filling a

particular role for a group. A role is a function needed for the operating of a group. It can be an "outer role," such as chairperson, secretary, treasurer, group member, and so on. They are the official positions a group assigns people to make sure the group operates smoothly. Outer roles must be filled and they can be filled by a variety of people.

In addition to outer roles are "inner roles." Inner roles maintain the emotional life and health of the group. (Some examples include a peacemaker who calms things down, an initiator who gets things going, a disturber who stirs things up, a clown who infuses light-heartedness, a time-keeper who keeps the group on track, a warm-heart who brings tenderness.) A relationship needs those and many more inner roles to be filled for the group to work effectively and satisfyingly. Much like outer roles, inner roles can be filled by anyone, as long as the role is filled.

In both cases roles are functions and not people. But, we often forget that and think that people are their roles. We then begin to cast people, or they cast themselves in those same roles over and over again, especially if it is a natural fit. A newly formed group, where people know each other, tend to know who is a natural for the different official outer roles. Joe makes a good chairperson. Sally makes a good secretary. Jane is good at recording information on chart paper. John does a great job with opening and closing prayers. Unknowingly filling the roles with the "naturals" subtly biases the group to replicate their experiences in other groups with the same cast of characters. With the same cast, expect similar results.

Likewise with inner roles, the cast of characters can easily form. Alice is the peacemaker. Jim picks up on subtle feelings. Debra pushes to get things moving when we bog down. These roles are not official roles assigned by the group; however, people tend to expect individuals to play their usual roles. And individuals step into them easily because of natural inclinations. People fill them without even thinking and others automatically count on that function being carried by those persons.

Over time, people get tired of being the one who is always responsible for keeping things on track, offering the prayer, saying what no one else wants to admit, and so on. That is what we mean by role nausea. At that point, it is time for the group to talk about roles and remind themselves that people are not their roles. Switching roles can effect growth in individuals and bring new energy and ideas into the group.

As your group talks about roles and which the members will fill, use curiosity. Become curious about yourself and a role you might like to "try on." Become curious about the not-so-visible strengths others may have. Review the section "Developing Curiosity" in chapter 3 and practice asking curiosity questions.

Q. *I honestly don't like conflict and I want to avoid it. Is there an easy way for me to deal with conflict?*

A. Conflict is uncomfortable for many people. Conflict is that moment where multiple ideas are present at the same time and bumping up against each other. That is the pool from which arises new thoughts, new ideas, and new growth. Conflict is that chaotic space in which God creates, so it behooves us to learn how to be present with conflict and even appreciate it.

People usually talk about conflict management. The phrase itself paints a particular picture. Conflict is something "not good" that must be "managed." While that is one perspective on conflict, we invite you to try on ours—that conflict is a creative moment where God can help new things happen.

Conflict signals that people care. It indicates that people are alive and invested in what is happening and are willing to expend their energy on it. And who doesn't welcome invested and energetic people! Whenever change is initiated in a congregation, conflict generally emerges, often in the form of resistance. Resistance provides valuable information about the interests and values that people fear will be ignored.

Before we can hear the interests and values the upset person or persons are trying to convey in their words and actions, we have to be able to listen. That means exercising the foundational skills of self-awareness, self-management, and social awareness outlined in chapters 1 through 3 of this book.

Think about conflict as the place where God will be present and new understandings and ways of doing things will emerge. Get curious. Begin to look for the important and useful information being offered to you. What leads that person to be so invested and put so much energy into the issue? What interest or value is being stepped on? Put your effort into getting to know this person in deeper and new ways.

Becoming curious serves both us and the team. First, we benefit by stepping out of the role of the one being attacked to being a curious explorer. This provides the distance to see that the something being attacked is separate from us. Then we can become curious about what that "thing" is that is so threatening to the person, seeking to understand it from that person's perspective. Look for those interests and values that the person senses are threatened by the proposal. A shift usually takes place when the other person senses us shifting from defensiveness or combativeness to caring curiosity.

Listening to and understanding the other person creates a deeper bond between us and them. It brings to light valuable information and insight, cueing us to important things to which we were oblivious. A new voice is heard or a voice is heard more fully. With that voice the team gains a fuller view of reality and its work becomes more effective.

Q. *I'm an associate pastor in a larger church. The congregation thinks everything's fine between the senior pastor and me, but in reality it's terrible. He yells at the staff, demeans us during staff meetings, and generally makes life miserable. How am I supposed to love someone like that?*

A. Loving someone does not mean letting that person walk all over you. A loving response honors God, the other person, and yourself. In light of that, sometimes the loving response is to say, "Stop. I can't be with you when you speak this way to me." This says, in essence, I will not collude with you by condoning your behavior with my presence. Take a time out from each other until things cool down. Some relationships can be brought into healthy alignment when clear requests are made and stronger boundaries are set.

When a relationship becomes toxic, it exhibits the almost continual presence of what John Gottman terms the "Four Horsemen of the Apocalypse": criticism, contempt, defensiveness, or stonewalling (see chapter 4). They rarely appear alone. One person's use of one of those stances will typically call out that or another one of the stances in the other person. Criticism and contempt tend to evoke defensiveness and stonewalling, creating cycles that are difficult to stop. For relationships trapped in such a cycle, stepping away and leaving the relationship may be the only solution.

Q. *The groups I am in tend to have strong, vocal people. They seem to be clear about what they want and the positions they take. What difference do I as a quieter person really make?*

A. A favorite painting of ours is *Christ's Entry into Brussels in 1889.* The artist, James Ensor, depicts a circus-like crowd of people moving down a street. The mass is made up of smaller knots of people, each marching to their own drummer, full of themselves and their own interests. They seem nearly oblivious to what's happening around them or even being part of a bigger group.

At the center of the painting, hardly visible, is Jesus, alone on a donkey. Only those closest to him notice him. They alone look transfixed by awe. The painting poses the common human question: "How does one person make a difference in a fragmented world?" Ensor seems to offer an answer: "By reaching out and touching those you are next to. Focus on what is possible rather than being overwhelmed by the impossible."

We as individuals impact groups more than we imagine. The attitudes and feelings we bring with us into a room affect the group and its work. Therefore, the starting place is always with ourselves as described in chapter 4: "Learning to

Love." (See especially exercises 4.1, 4.2, and 4.3.) What perspective will we hold? What is our high dream for what might happen? How will we view and hold the other team members during the meeting?

We subtly shape a group when we embody how we want the group to be and function. Speaking authentically and listening respectfully encourage others too. When a person overcomes a natural hesitance or fear to speak, it sends a strong signal to a group. Speaking in a quiet and simple way from our heart can have a profound effect. Groups that are used to people taking and defending positions are often stopped in their tracks by such a comment. We have watched large and powerful groups shift through the sincere heartfelt statement of one quiet person.

Model the skills of loving relationship in chapter 4 and your impact will be greater than the loudest and most vocal person. Start in simply ways and focus on what is possible.

Q. *I've been asked to lead a new group being formed in our congregation. How do we get off on the right foot?*

A. We offer three pieces of advice:

1. Pay attention to relationships.
2. Make sure you, as the leader, have clarity about what you have been asked to do.
3. Once formed, let the group take on its own life.

Addressing relationships is central. How do you want people to relate to each other? We assume your desire is for right relationships. For the group to form in a way that embodies right relationships, it all begins with you. Your attitudes and behavior provide the model for the group. Right from the beginning, embody the essential qualities. A good structure for your preparation is using chapter 4: "Learning to Love." Use the six essential questions as you picture in your mind each participant in the group. Use the first three questions as you picture in your mind the group as a whole. Remember that the degree to which the group embodies love depends heavily on the extent you embody love. Be clear about and hold for yourself your high dream for the group. Know, too, your low dream of what you fear might happen, and take care not to feed it.

Second, make sure you understand the purpose for the group's formation and any outcomes that might be expected. If the group is forming at your initiative, be clear in your own mind on why you called the group together and what your expectations are. Perhaps the formation of the group was someone else's idea and you have been asked to lead it. Pastors, staff people, and committees sometimes gather a group with a particular hope in mind. Those hopes may be vague without any real thought of the specific task given to the group. Do not gather a group without first clarifying for yourself why they are gathered. Find out what is being asked of you and of them. Then, clearly communicate what is in your mind to the others. Once you gather the team, spend time as a group defining the group's purpose and developing a mutual understanding of the fuller meaning of your task. (See exercise 5.1.)

Third, be prepared to let go of all your attempts to manipulate the group. This involves both their decisions around how they will structure their life together and the outcome of their work. The underlying belief that God works powerfully and creatively in and through groups has led to the gathering of your group. Groups, once formed, take on a life of their own. Trust that God will work and know that, in many respects, what emerges is out of your hands.

Q. *My team is responsible for only a small piece of the total life and program of the congregation. We have surfaced the values that guide our team's work. Why do we need to also be aware of the values of the congregation? How do we discover what the congregation's values are? How do we use them once we find them?*

A. No team within the church is an independent, autonomous group. Each exists as an integral part of and in service to the mission and vision of the congregation as a whole.

Mission and vision statements provide a rich source for identifying declared values. Ask of each part of the statement: "What is the value the congregation holds that makes this part of the mission and vision important for us?" The answers to the question give a list of the congregation's declared values. The list reflects what we honor when we fully, as a congregation, live the way we want to live.

Identified values actually serve us only to the extent they are used. The following suggests a simply, practical way to allow them to inform and guide decisions. After your group has discerned which values will guide your work (see exercise 5.2), post them on the wall when you meet. For the purpose of discussion, let's say you are a worship committee with three values: authentic message, artistic beauty, and warm fellowship. As you come to every decision point, you would ask yourselves questions such as: "How well does this solution honor our value of presenting an authentic message? Artistic beauty? Warm fellowship?" The group would look for ways to make sure every aspect of worship honored those values. Evaluations would seek to assess how well they were being embodied.

On another part of the wall, always keep posted the values of the congregation. Again, for the purpose of discussion, let's say that among those values are inclusiveness, God centered, and honoring the sacredness of each person. The group will want to reflect on ways that their plans live out and embody these values of the congregation.

Your small piece of the whole makes all the difference in the world. The whole is more than merely the sum of the parts; however, the whole is dependent on each part playing it's own unique role in living out the mission and vision of the congregation.

We are interested in hearing your stories and questions. How have you furthered right relationship in your settings? What are you learning about yourself, relationships, and God as you do this work? What tools have you discovered and found helpful? What do you still puzzle over? We invite you to share your learnings, your stories, and your questions with us. E-mail us at courageousspace@aol.com.

Epilogue | # Our Work Is World Work

O n Sunday, May 18, 1980, Mount Saint Helens spewed tons of ash into the sky over the state of Washington. Days later ash from Mount Saint Helens had traveled the miles around the earth, returning to the atmosphere over the erupted volcano. The ash from that one spot in Washington affected the atmosphere and life in every place on earth. Some areas experienced the results of the eruption in a dramatic way, others hardly at all, but no place on earth remained unaffected.

Similarly, the relationship shared by a team within a congregation affects relationships in the entire congregation. The relationship shared by a congregation affects the community in which it is located and thus the world beyond. The ripples set off by that one small team are felt around the whole world. Our work affects far more than those we reach out and physically touch. Our relationships and our openness to be a channel for God's work touches all of creation no less than a volcano erupting in Washington. Our "ash" influences the entire atmosphere and all of life. The effect, traveling the globe, returns then to affect us.

The ecological interrelatedness of all of creation makes our work world work. Faithfulness to God calls us to form right relationships and offer them for God's use. Through our relationships, the kindom of God permeates creation and becomes a lived experience for people.

God's Dreaming for the World

The Hebrew and Christian scriptures present a God who is concerned with the well-being of the world and who works for its wholeness. The most ancient of our scriptures have God proclaiming, "My work is world work." In Genesis, God declares to Abram God's all-encompassing intent. Promising blessing to Abram and his family, God claims Abram as a channel for much bigger work. "In you [or by you] all the families of the earth shall be blessed" (Gen. 12:3). God chose Abram and established a covenantal partnership. The job of that partnership was to carry out a dream for all of creation.

The Christian scriptures end with a picture of that dream, a vision of a new Jerusalem, a holy city. The vision portrays God dwelling with people in a place of creative peace and fulfillment (Rev. 21:1-4). The world work of God finds its completion in bringing the fullness of God's dream into concrete reality.

How do we get from the intent declared to Abram to the fulfillment depicted in Revelation? How do we get from God's dream to the transformation of all of creation? Like Abram, God invites us into covenantal partnership. Through us and our convenantal relationships, creation edges along from the intent shared with Abram to the vision depicted in Revelation.

Our choices impact creation. Through creating and offering right relationship as a vehicle for God's work, the world shifts toward fulfillment of God's dream. To remain an effective and willing channel for God's dreaming requires we be open to God's continual influence in our relationships.

Open to the Reinfluencing of God

As partners of God we work to remain open to God's influencing. We do this through a variety of ways, including prayer, study, discernment, and a true desire to act in ways consistent with God's will. When we or the groups we are part of get a glimpse of the path God offers us, it sparks our dreaming and our commitment. We align ourselves and our resources. We give ourselves wholeheartedly to the work. The result for our congregations and for the people we seek to serve is health and wholeness.

When we experience being a channel for God's working in a particular way, it is easy for us to become attached to being used in that particular way. Sometimes we hang on to work past its time of being needed by God to bring health and wholeness to others. In such instance, the work, devoid of God's Spirit, grows hollow and burdensome to us. But memories of how important it used to be to us and to others keep us from letting go.

Congregations exist for a holy purpose: to mediate God's love and grace and be a continually open channel for God's work. What God requires of us will shift across time and circumstance. Our task is to remain open and responsive, available for God's use. This will require we let go of things that have become near and dear to us and willingly give ourselves to God to be reinfluenced, reformed, and reused. "Just like the clay in the potter's hand, so are you in my hand, O house of Israel" (Jer. 18:6b).

One Congregation's Story

For several years, a priority of developing caring relationships among members had guided the work of St. Luke's. Life together had been divisive and fractured. So, convinced of the need, people gave themselves and their resources to create a model of caring community in their congregation. People traveled miles to participate, motivated by their appreciation of and commitment to the relationships they formed there. Continually, people would mention how transformational those relationships were to them. Success had removed the urgency of crisis they experienced a decade earlier, and life together was sweet.

And then, some in the congregation began to develop an awareness of the changes taking place in the neighborhood surrounding the church. They noticed an increase in immigrant families and low-income single-parent households—demographic groups very different from those who currently attended St. Luke's. Holding on to the bigger picture of why they existed, the congregation made a brave and faithful decision. Their work had not ended, but was just beginning. They would use this new and sweet place they lived in as a platform from which to now turn and do something totally new. They allowed themselves to be reinfluenced by God for the sake of God's work.

Many of the newer families in the neighborhood either did not attend any church or traveled out of the neighborhood to more homogeneous congregations. Many of the congregation's families traveled to St. Luke's to be with people just like themselves. St. Luke's began to sense God dreaming something new through them. How could neighbors so different from each other learn to live together—not just as a geographic community but as a community of care and love? The congregation began to sense more strongly God's dream of the kindom for the world. And, they began to sense their call to be an embodiment of that kindom.

God's world work invites us to remove the walls and gates from our beloved communities. World work calls us to expand our circles, including additional parts of God's world into our relationships. Expanding the circle and including others churns up the patterns of our present relationships. Continual realignment and the development of new covenant agreements become a regular part of life. But we give ourselves to the work, knowing it is God's work. We give ourselves, our relationship, as a channel for God's kindom to fill the earth.

Beginning Where We Are but Not Stopping There

We can find ourselves enamored of a grand and glorious dream, but resist the daily work that leads to the fulfillment of that dream. "I love humanity; it's people I can't stand." We commit to nothing less than the grand dream of the kindom extending throughout the world. In this era of war, our hearts, minds, and souls long for right relationship to permeate all of creation. Our circle of concern, and certainly God's, includes the entire earth; however, the journey to the fulfillment of those dreams begins today with how we relate to others in our daily interactions.

Where does our world work begin this week? The list includes all within our circle of influence—any person in our home; any person we face across the counter in a store; any person in our workplace, our recreational and social gatherings; any person we sit across from in a committee meeting; any person we are with in worship. These are the ones God gives to us to create right relationship with right now. Through our daily relationships we will impact other people and thus the world in ways we cannot begin to imagine. Our relationships create the ash that changes everything.

Resources

Arbinger Institute. *Leadership and Self-Deception: Getting Out of the Box.* San Francisco: Berrett-Koehler, 2000.

Childre, Doc, and Howard Martin. *The Heartmath Solution: The Institute of HeartMath's Revolutionary Program for Engaging the Power of the Heart's Intelligence.* San Francisco: HarperSanFrancisco, 1999.

Goleman, Daniel. *Working with Emotional Intelligence.* New York: Bantam Books, 1998.

Goleman, Daniel, Richard Boyatzis, and Annie McKee. *Primal Leadership: Realizing the Power of Emotional Intelligence.* Boston: Harvard Business School Press, 2002.

Gottman, John. *Why Marriages Succeed or Fail: And How You Can Make Yours Last.* New York: Simon & Schuster, 1994.

Gottman, John, and Nan Silver. *The Seven Principles for Making Marriage Work: A Practical Guide from the Country's Foremost Relationship Expert.* New York: Three Rivers Press, 1999.

Heifetz, Ronald A., and Marty Linsky. *Leadership on the Line: Staying Alive through the Dangers of Leading.* Boston: Harvard Business School Press, 2002.

Kotter, John P., and Dan S. Cohen. *The Heart of Change: Real-Life Stories of How People Change Their Organizations.* Boston: Harvard Business School Press, 2002.

Melander, Rochelle, and Harold Eppley. *Growing Together: Spiritual Exercises for Church Committees*. Minneapolis: Augsburg Fortress, 1998.

————. *The Spiritual Leader's Guide to Self-Care*. Bethesda, Md.: The Alban Institute, 2002.

Mindell, Amy. *The Spiritual Art of Metaskills*. Portland, Ore.: Lao Tse Press, 1995.

Mindell, Arnold. *The Deep Democracy of Open Forums: Practical Steps to Conflict Prevention and Resolution for the Family, Workplace, and World*. Charlottesville, Va.: Hampton Roads Publishing Company, 2002.

————. *The Dreammaker's Apprentice: Using Heightened States of Consciousness to Interpret Dreams*. Charlottesville, Va.: Hampton Roads Publishing Company, 2001.

Olsen, Charles M. *Transforming Church Boards into Communities of Spiritual Leaders*. Bethesda, Md.: The Alban Institute, 1995.

Owen, Harrison. *The Power of Spirit: How Organizations Transform*. San Francisco: Berrett-Koehler, 2000.

Patterson, Kerry, Joseph Grenny, Ron McMillan, and Al Switzler. *Crucial Conversations: Tools for Talking When Stakes Are High*. New York: McGraw-Hill, 2002.

Quinn, Robert E. *Change the World: How Ordinary People Can Achieve Extraordinary Results*. San Francisco: Jossey-Bass, 2000.

Sellon, Mary K., Daniel P. Smith, and Gail E. Grossman. *Redeveloping the Congregation: A How-To for Lasting Change*. Bethesda, Md.: The Alban Institute, 2002.

Tolle, Eckhart. *The Power of NOW*. Novato, Calif.: New World Library, 1999.

Wheatley, Margaret J. *Turning to One Another: Simple Conversations to Restore Hope to the Future*. San Francisco: Berrett-Koehler, 2002.

Wheatley, Margaret J., and Myron Kellner-Rogers. *A Simpler Way*. San Francisco: Berrett-Koehler, 1996.

Whitworth, Laura, Henry Kimsey-House, and Phil Sandahl. *Coactive Coaching: New Skills for Coaching People toward Success in Work and Life*, Palo Alto, Calif.: Davies-Black Publishing, 1998.